NAPOLEON III

AND THE
SECOND EMPIRE

NAPOLEON III

and the

Second Empire

J. P. T. BURY

Corpus Christi College
Cambridge

THE ENGLISH UNIVERSITIES PRESS LTD
ST PAUL'S HOUSE WARWICK LANE
LONDON EC4

SBN 340 05858 7

Second impression 1970

The English Universities Press Ltd
St Paul's House, Warwick Lane, London EC4

Printed and bound in Great Britain by
Hazell Watson & Viney Ltd
Aylesbury, Bucks

Introduction to the Series

This series has been undertaken in the conviction that no subject is more important than history. For though the conquests of natural science (nuclear fission, the exploration of space, genetic advance, bacteriology, etc.) have given their character to the age, it is actually a greater need to gain control of the forces of nature loosed upon us. The prime urgency, the deepest necessity is in the human field: to understand the nature and condition of man as a pre-condition of better controls, and fewer disasters, in the world of politics and society.

There is no better introduction to this sphere, and the understanding of its problems, than history. *Some* knowledge of history, we feel, ought to prevent some mistakes: at every point we can learn vicariously from the experience of others before us.

To take one point only – the understanding of politics: how can we understand the world of affairs around us, if we do not know how it came to be what it is? How to interpret the United States, or Soviet Russia, France, Germany or Britain without some knowledge of their history?

Some evidence of the growing awareness of this may be seen in the great increase of interest in history among the general public, and in the much larger place the subject has come to take in education.

The most congenial, as well as the most concrete and practical, approach to history is the biographical: through the lives of great men whose careers have been significant in history. Fashions in historical writing have their ups and downs; men's and women's lives have their

perennial interest – though in this series we are chiefly
concerned to show their historical significance, the contribution they made to their age: *Men and their Times.*

A generation ago historical biographies were rather
unfashionable with analytical historians and technicians,
like Namier: he ended by writing scores of miniature
biographies of M.P.s. The detailed analysis of Civil War
and Commonwealth has ended by showing that there
were almost as many party-divisions as there were individuals. We are back in the realm of biography and the
biographical approach to history, since there is no greater
diversity, variety and subtlety than in the lives of individual men and women, particularly those who left a
mark on their time.

A. L. ROWSE

OXFORD

Preface

LOUIS NAPOLEON BONAPARTE, later Emperor of the French as Napoleon III, had a career more romantic in its course, more dramatic in its tragedy, and more momentous in its impact upon Europe than any other sovereign who ruled between 1815 and 1914. His enigmatic character and the contradictions in his policies can never fail to fascinate and men will not cease to argue about his intentions and whether or not his rule was preponderantly beneficent or calamitous to his country and to Europe as a whole. With these wider implications this small survey cannot, however, be more than incidentally concerned. It is not easy to convey in so brief a space the full richness and complexity of a career which impinged upon so many aspects of human activity in so many parts of the world. I have, however, tried in particular to illustrate the nature and consistency of Napoleon's ideas by frequent reference to his own writings and utterances, and, although foreign policy must inevitably loom large in any study of his reign, I have endeavoured to give more space than has sometimes been usual to economic issues and to Napoleon's interests overseas.

J. P. T. B.

Contents

Maps

Chapter One

The Nephew of the Emperor

'IF the destiny which my birth promised me had not been changed by circumstances,' wrote Prince Louis Napoleon Bonaparte in 1840, 'as nephew of the Emperor I should have been one of the defenders of his throne, one of the propagators of his ideas; the glory would have been mine to form one of the pillars of his edifice or to die in one of the squares of his Guards fighting for France.'

'The destiny which my birth promised me'; 'nephew of the Emperor'; 'fighting for France'. These words are key words for the early history of Louis Napoleon. No man was ever to be more conscious of the 'destiny' of his birth, no nephew to exploit more skilfully his kinship with a man of genius, no exile to seize with more alacrity any opportunity to proclaim his desire to serve and fight for France. Yet it was in keeping with a career that was often to puzzle historians as much as contemporaries that even his birth itself, or rather its legitimacy, should have been questioned. The charge of illegitimacy has, however, never been substantiated. What gave it credibility was the unhappy separation of his parents, the moody and neurasthenic Louis Bonaparte, King of Holland, and the artistic, sociable and flirtatious Hortense de Beauharnais, daughter of the Empress Josephine. Their marriage had characteristic-ally been ordained by Napoleon, who was Louis' elder brother, but they had soon become estranged and Louis Napoleon, their third and youngest son, born on April 20, 1808, was the issue of a purely temporary reconciliation. A year later Louis was vainly asking the imperial family to allow his divorce. A year later still, after a quarrel with the Emperor, he abdicated the Dutch throne and retired to live mainly in Germany or Italy. His withdrawal meant that, to all intents and purposes,

Louis Napoleon during his early years was fatherless. Perhaps the boy inherited a certain moodiness, taciturnity and un-doubted obstinacy from his father, but it was Hortense, not Louis, who would be the dominant figure in his formative years.

Thus, Louis Napoleon was born a prince, though of upstart royalty, and spent his first years in palaces and amid imperial splendour. He had, moreover, been born in Paris and passed his early childhood in France, so that, for all his long years of subsequent exile, he could truly claim to be a Frenchman* as well as nephew of the Emperor. Indeed, Napoleon had in 1809 decreed that his nephews should not be allowed to leave the country; and even after the birth in 1811 of his son, the King of Rome, later known as the Duc de Reichstadt, the Emperor continued to take a lively interest in Hortense's two surviving children, Napoleon Louis and Louis Napoleon, hoping no doubt that they would indeed grow to be 'pillars of his edifice'.

'Circumstances' in the shape of the Allied armies decreed otherwise. The overthrow of the Emperor and his removal from the European scene changed the destiny of all the Bonapartes. Louis Napoleon saw his uncle for the last time in 1815 when he was only seven; and when Napoleon died in 1821 at St. Helena grieved 'not to have seen him once before his death, for', he admitted, 'in Paris I was so young that I scarcely have any remembrance of him except in my heart'. The coherent image of the Emperor that Louis Napoleon built for himself was largely posthumous, fashioned in exile and not in France.

This first period of exile lasted for the best part of fifteen years. After Waterloo, Hortense and her children were given passports for Switzerland. In January 1816 a law passed by the Restoration Government in Paris condemned all the Bona-partes to perpetual banishment from France. In the Europe of Legitimate Monarchy they were suspect persons, liable to police surveillance in whatever country they found themselves.

The path of exile was not easy for an ex-Queen with an absentee husband. For Hortense it was all the harder because

---

* Thanking his electors in 1848, he was to call himself a child of Paris.

a tribunal had recently awarded Louis the custody of his elder son, Napoleon Louis, now ten years old, and it was during the first stages of their journey that Louis' agent came to claim the brother to whom Louis Napoleon was devoted. Thus, when he was only seven, much of the remainder of Louis Napoleon's small world came toppling down: his uncle was dethroned and banished, he and his mother were refugees, his only brother was taken from him. Nor could his mother immediately find a new and permanent home. When Geneva refused to allow her refuge and Savoy proved unsafe, she and her modest entourage stayed for a while at Constance in the Grand Duchy of Baden. But the Baden authorities, too, were afraid of giving lasting asylum to the wife of a Bonaparte and refused to allow her to buy a property in the Grand Duchy. It was not until 1817 that she was able to purchase in the canton of Thurgau in Switzerland the small Château of Arenenberg which was to be her main home and Louis Napoleon's until her death there twenty years later.

The education of Louis Napoleon was in consequence dependent largely upon his mother's choice of home and tutors, upon her cult of the past, her restlessness, and upon his own will-power and inclinations. It was the education of an exiled prince with moderate means and no prospect of a throne. Circumstances made it a cosmopolitan upbringing against the background of a French household in exile. Accordingly, when Louis Napoleon returned to France he was exceptional among Frenchmen of his generation in being master of three foreign languages and in not having had the legal training so usual with French politicians. But, though it was achieved mainly in German-speaking lands, his education was basically French and this was no less important than Louis Napoleon's birth and early childhood in France.

The formal part of this upbringing, apart from later military training with the Swiss artillery at Thun, ended in 1827. Hortense had the wisdom to choose French tutors for her son, though the choice was singular. The first, the Abbé Bertrand, was an excellent man, but neither a teacher nor a disciplinarian. When, after their long separation, Louis Bonaparte met his son again at Leghorn in 1818, he was shocked by his demeanour and made it clear to Hortense that a new tutor ought to be found. When the new tutor came in 1819 he discovered his pupil to be a nervous and delicate child, 'backward, ignorant and lazy . . . at twelve [sic] years of age he might be no more than seven'. The new tutor, Philippe Le Bas, was a man of very different character from his predecessor. It is remarkable that Louis and Hortense both selected French Republicans to have charge of their sons' education, as though deliberately to justify the Bonapartes' claim to be heirs of the French Revolution. Vieillard and Armandi, tutors to Napoleon Louis in Italy, were Republicans or Liberals in sympathy. Le Bas was the son of a regicide deputy of the Convention, who had been a close friend of Robespierre, and himself, too, professed Republican and anti-clerical views. How far these views influenced his pupil we have no sure means of knowing, but it is a reasonable surmise that his radicalism played some part in broadening the sympathies of a boy who was already generous by nature. What mattered immediately, however, was that Le Bas was above all a scholar, a conscientious teacher and a good disciplinarian, who quickly won the respect and affection of his pupil. Louis Napoleon was now belatedly, but not too late, made to know what it was to work.

By 1821 the boy was ready for something more and his mother took a house at Augsburg in Bavaria where Louis Napoleon continued to study under Le Bas' direction, but also for a time attended the local *Gymnasium* as a day boy. This regime appears to have continued with some variations and interruptions for the best part of six years until, in 1827, Le Bas was dismissed on the grounds of economy. By then, however, his work was largely done. The delicate and backward child of whom he had taken charge had grown into a physically courageous and active young man of nineteen, an excellent horseman, a strong swimmer and a good shot. Moreover, although a fundamental disposition to indolence remained, he had learnt how to work when he wished, and there had been aroused in him an intellectual curiosity which enabled him to continue his own education in periods of enforced leisure and which, when he was Emperor, distinguished him above most of his fellow sovereigns. This curiosity was above all historical and political, military and mechanical; he was a visionary among rulers, but a visionary with a practical bent.

In the meantime, less formal influences had also been at work in his upbringing, the influences of Arenenberg and Italy. The atmosphere of Arenenberg was rarefied, for here Hortense surrounded herself with relics of the Imperial past and the image of the Emperor was ubiquitous. Books, furniture, and pictures all recalled the old days of splendour. To Arenenberg, too, came visitors who remembered the Emperor and had served his regime, Hortense's brother, Eugène de Beauharnais, her quondam lover Charles de Flahaut, by whom in 1811 she had had a child, one day to be celebrated as the Duc de Morny, and many others. So here the Empire and the role of the Bonapartes could never be forgotten and Louis Napoleon was taught always to remember who he was. The Bonapartes, his mother told him, were undergoing a painful reversal of fortune, but times might change . . . 'Because of your name you will always be something either in Europe or in the New World—never lose hope. Always be on the look-out for favourable opportunities. If France escapes you for good, Italy, Germany, Russia or England would still give you resources in the future. Everywhere one can conceive of turns of fortune which can raise the heir of a great and famous name to the clouds . . . You and your brother are, after the King of Rome, the heirs of Napoleon.'

From 1823 onwards Italy also came to play an important part in Louis Napoleon's life. Here most of the Bonapartes had taken refuge. His father and his brother, Napoleon Louis, had settled in Florence; his grandmother, Madame Mère, and her other children had been granted asylum in Rome by the Pope, and in Rome in 1825 Hortense had been given the use of the beautiful Villa Paolina. So visits to Italy, especially in the winter, became more frequent, to the detriment of Louis Napoleon's studies and the despair of Le Bas. But this new association with the land where his uncle Napoleon had first made his name, where his uncle Eugène had been Viceroy, and which was now the home of so many of his relations was of deep and lasting significance. Not only did he here enjoy a new and more lively social and amorous life, but here he formed friendships with young Italian Liberals such as Francesco Arese and became involved in conspiracies which profoundly affected his future career.

In July 1830, when he was for the first time following an artillery course in camp at Thun, revolution in Paris swept the Bourbons from the French throne and established the more Liberal monarchy of the House of Orléans. But any hopes the Bonapartes might have cherished of return to France were soon disappointed, for in September the French Chamber of Deputies re-enacted the banishment law of 1816. The July Revolution, however, had encouraged the restlessness and aspirations of liberals and revolutionaries elsewhere, including Italy. The death of Pope Pius VIII on November 30 increased tension in Rome, where the authorities convinced themselves that the Bonapartists were scheming to take advantage of the interregnum, raise the standard of revolt and proclaim Louis Napoleon as Regent for the King of Rome. The degree of Louis Napoleon's complicity in this somewhat shadowy and abortive plot remains in doubt. But he and others were expelled the city. He immediately joined his brother in Florence, and the Roman affair was but the prelude to a new and more serious adventure.

By the beginning of February 1831 parts of Central Italy were in insurrection and Louis Napoleon and his brother Napoleon Louis went off to join the rebels. The escapade, deplored by his mother, who saw its perils, and condemned by his father and uncles, was a brief and tragic but momentous experience for the future Emperor. There is no evidence for the oft-repeated story that, like his brother, he was a member of the Carbonari; but in the rising he had associated himself with what, in a letter published in France soon after, he called 'the sacred cause of Italian independence', and he had made a demonstration against the old regimes. 'The name we bear', Louis Napoleon wrote to his mother, 'obliges us to help the unfortunate peoples who are calling for our aid'. In the rising he had his first experience of active rebellion. In it he lost his dearly loved brother, who died of measles, possibly following a wound, at Forli. As a result of it he became a hunted man, rescued from capture and probable imprisonment, if not death, by the courage and ingenuity of his mother, who set out to join him and contrived his escape with the aid of a British passport and various disguises across Northern Italy into France and, eventually, England.

The decision to brave the French Government's ban and to enter France was a bold one, but Hortense hoped for indulgence from Louis Philippe, whom she had befriended in 1815, while Louis Napoleon drafted a letter in which he appealed to the King to allow him to serve in the French army, here for the first time formally putting forward his claim to fight for France. In a secret meeting Louis Philippe received Hortense most kindly, but it was not possible to come to any arrangement whereby the ban on the exiles could be removed. Not unnaturally the Orleanist Government could contemplate this only in return for their allegiance to the July Monarchy and for this Louis Napoleon was still less prepared than his mother. So when a Bonapartist demonstration took place in the Place Vendôme in Paris on May 5, the tenth anniversary of the death of the Emperor, the authorities hastened the departure of these unwelcome visitors. A few days later they landed in England and Louis Napoleon set eyes for the first time on the country which he was often to visit, whose ally he was to become, and in which he was to die. This first visit lasted only three months, but was long enough for him to make useful acquaintances in English society, in which one day he would be still more at home than among the aristocracy of Rome. At the end of their stay the refugees received passports from the French Government which enabled them to return unmolested to Switzerland, and before the summer of 1831 was over they were back at Arenenberg.

The five years from 1831 to 1836 have been called the least eventful of Louis Napoleon's life, but if they were undramatic they were none the less of crucial importance, for it was in them that he began to cast himself for the role of Pretender. His anxious mother, after such a troubled year, now hoped that her one surviving son might marry and settle down in comfortable exile, quietly awaiting any favourable change in the wind of fortune. In other circumstances perhaps he would have been content to do so. But the loss of his brother and other experiences of 1831 made him a changed man, one no longer content with the happinesses of a private citizen but a man with a mission, convinced that the destiny of his birth had given him an active political role to play and that France was to be the scene. Accordingly, the 'young hero' refused an invitation from a Polish mission (August 1831) to lead an expedition to help the Polish insurgents against Russia. Accordingly, though rumour might attribute to him designs on the throne of Belgium (June 1831) or the prospect of becoming King Consort of Portugal (1835), he categorically disclaimed any such intentions, stating that his chief desire was to serve his own country and making clear that that country was France. But serving France could not mean serving the Orleanist regime. He became instead its persistent foe, seeking every opportunity to bring about its overthrow. Those six weeks spent in France in 1831 on the way from Italy to England were all-important in making France and not Italy henceforward the focus of his ambition, for not only had he had the emotional experience of seeing Paris again, but he had had the opportunity to learn something of the opposition to the July Monarchy and probably to make contact with some of its Republican and Bonapartist members. When a Bonapartist demonstration had taken place under his very windows, he might well, if mistakenly, believe that there was a great body of opinion in France ready to back the Bonapartist cause, if only a leader could be found.

The way for his assumption of the role of Pretender was smoothed by the death of Napoleon's son, the young Duc de Reichstadt, in Austria in July 1832. Louis Napoleon's father and his uncles, comfortably settled in Italy or England, had no aspiration to be active claimants to the throne of France, and so, now that his elder brother too was dead, he could seize the Napoleonic heritage as his. But what did it amount to? The *Constitutionnel*, in an obituary of the Duc de Reichstadt on August 1, 1832, declared that 'Napoleon II had in France if not a party, at least numerous partisans. Here is a heritage which the factions are going to dispute among themselves and with the government and which will go to the man who knows how to rally the masses of the people to the true interests of the *patrie*.' In fact, after the death of 'Napoleon II', the danger of Bonapartism as a political force that could conceivably threaten the July Monarchy seemed to be receding. There was, as the *Constitutionnel* had indicated, no organized Bonapartist party, the revolutionary secret societies were tending to become more exclusively Republican, while the Government themselves sought to attract the goodwill and allegiance of Napoleon's devotees by permitting his statue to be re-erected on the column in the Place Vendôme in 1833, by completing the Arc de Triomphe which was 'inaugurated' in 1836, and finally by bringing back his ashes from St. Helena to the Invalides in 1840. But this was a risky game to play, as the Austrian Chancellor, Metternich, suggested; indeed Metternich, most experienced of European statesmen, had as early as 1832 told his ambassador in Paris to warn Louis Philippe concerning the successor to the Duc de Reichstadt: 'On the day of the Duke's death the young Louis Bonaparte will regard himself as called to the head of the French Republic.'

Metternich was, as often, perspicacious. Louis Napoleon, ostensibly living quietly in Switzerland as a Swiss citizen, doing his annual artillery training and writing about the problems of his adopted country—in 1833 he published a pamphlet entitled *Considérations politiques et militaires sur la Suisse* and in 1835 a substantial *Manuel d'Artillerie à l'usage des officiers suisses*—was in reality beginning to sketch a programme and to prepare a coup. Already before the death of the Duc de Reichstadt he had, in 1832, issued a slight brochure, entitled *Rêveries politiques*, in which he adumbrated ideas to be much more fully worked out in his most celebrated work, *Des Idées Napoléoniennes*. This clearly indicated his intention to exploit the legend already formulated by Napoleon himself at St. Helena, to build up the picture of a Liberal Empire based upon the principles of the Revolution and regenerating the peoples, and to rally Republicans as well as Bonapartists to his cause. Moreover, the same notion was skilfully, if incidentally, woven into the *Considérations politiques*, which concluded with a moving encomium on the great part played by former soldiers of the Empire on many European battle-fields. This and the *Manuel d'Artillerie*, copies of which he sent to many officers, served to enhance his reputation in Switzerland and showed not only that this young Bonaparte was well versed in the problems of the artillery, the arm in which Napoleon himself had specialized, but also that he at least was mindful of the reputation and greatness of the army of France.

Propaganda alone was, however, of little avail for an exiled prince with limited means. It was on the army and the people and the name of Napoleon that he rested his hopes. Had 'Napoleon II' appeared in Paris in 1830, he was convinced, the throne would have been his for the asking. So in October 1836 at Strasbourg with the aid of a handful of partisans, including a former officer called Fialin, better known as Persigny, who became one of his most faithful henchmen, he made the first of his bids for power. He trusted that the 'prestige of his name and the spell of his audacity' would win him the garrison of the city, some of whose officers were privy to the plot, and enable a triumphant march upon Paris, like that of Napoleon on his return from Elba. Had the Prince borne any resemblance to his famous uncle and not spoken French with a foreign accent, all might have gone well, at least at Strasbourg; but the plot miscarried when he was denounced by an officer as an impostor. One regiment only rallied and within two hours the Prince and his fellow-conspirators were prisoners. Shrewdly the Orleanist Government avoided making the ringleader a martyr and thus affording him the further publicity he was eager to gain. Instead of keeping him in long imprisonment or bringing him to trial they put him on a frigate bound for New York. A new period of exile had begun.

His stay in America was brief, for news of his mother's grave illness caused him to hurry back to Arenenberg, where he remained from August 1837 until her death in October. His inheritance from her estate now made him a comparatively wealthy man, free to keep a style befitting a pretender. Her death, however, meant the break-up of his old home. The French authorities were no longer minded to have such a conspirator on their doorstep and called for his expulsion from Switzerland. The Swiss authorities refused the demand and, when the French Government began to mass troops on the Swiss frontier, it looked as though Louis Napoleon was about to be the cause of a serious international incident. But, not for the last time, he knew when to make a graceful retreat. He voluntarily withdrew in the cause of peace, decided to make England his home, at least for a while, and eventually sold Arenenberg. Had the French Government persisted in seeking to impose its will by force, the Swiss citizen Louis Bonaparte would have been in an embarrassing position, not 'fighting for France' but an officer in the ranks of the enemy. Yet the *Gazette de France* might well ask what the July Monarchy had gained in having the Prince in England rather than in Switzerland, and might well point out that Paris was nearer to London than to Arenenberg!

The needy adventurer who had spent a short time in England in 1831, 1832 and 1837, now went back there again 'relatively rich and almost royal', with a suite of seven companions, including Conneau, long to be his doctor, and Vaudrey and Persigny two of his fellow conspirators at Strasbourg. 'Louis Napoleon', said a paper called *L'Europe Industrielle* at the end of October 1838, announcing his retirement to England, 'is no longer a Swiss citizen—he is Napoleon III—a new pretender.' He did in fact go as a celebrity after all the publicity he had recently enjoyed and he was much lionized in English society. But what was remarkable was that he was more than ever the Pretender, undeterred by failure at Strasbourg which, many people thought, had made him ridiculous. Bulwer Lytton the novelist noted that the Prince had 'that intense faith in his own destiny with which men rarely fail of achieving something great'. 'Only think of that young man Louis Napoleon', said Lord Burghersh, 'nothing can persuade him he is not to be Emperor of France; this Strasbourg affair has not in the least shaken him; he is thinking constantly of what he is to do when on the throne.' And so it was; or rather he was thinking still more of how to acquire the throne, developing his programme, working many hours in the British Museum on the preparation of his *Des Idées Napoléoniennes*, and plotting yet another coup in France itself.

Des Idées Napoléoniennes, first published in 1839, was the most successful of his early works. It went through a number of editions and sold half a million copies before 1848. Brief, clear, and often eloquent, it portrayed Napoleon as 'the Messiah of the new ideas', which shone out like lighthouses amidst storms and darkness, a Napoleon whose goals were liberty, the independence of France, lasting peace in Europe and the establishment of a European confederation of nations, a Napoleon whose power rested on the whole mass of the nation, whose interests were the same as those of the people, who organized his country on the principles of equality, order, and justice. This was an Emperor who cared for agriculture as well as industry and commerce, and who was as wise and tolerant in his political as in his administrative organization of French affairs. The Napoleonic idea (he sometimes used the singular) was 'not an idea of war, but a social, an industrial, a commercial and humanitarian idea.' Last, but not least, the Prince skilfully suggested that those ideas represented the future, that they were 'everywhere in germ' and that they were 'advancing of their own momentum' although their author was dead. 'The system of the Emperor will be reconstituted of itself, sovereigns and people all will help it to re-establish itself.'

In a new foreword to a reissue of *Des Idées* in 1840 the author remarked that it was not only the ashes of the Emperor but his ideas which must be brought back to France. He was in fact already preparing to take them back and to be master of France in time himself to receive the ashes whose restoration the Orleanist Government had just arranged. In August he set out with a motley but intensely loyal crew from Gravesend to bring off at Boulogne the coup he had failed to achieve at Strasbourg. But this venture was still more of a fiasco. 'Louis Napoleon', recorded Disraeli (who later characterized the Prince and his mother as Florestan and Agrippina in his novel *Endymion*), 'who last year . . . nearly drowned us by his bad rowing, has now upset himself at Boulogne. Never was anything so rash and crude to all appearances as this "invasion", for he was joined by none.' This was not far from the truth, and forty-eight hours after their expedition had started the Prince and his companions were prisoners once more. This time the authorities were not so lenient. His trial before the Chamber of Peers brought him indeed much additional publicity, but his sentence was severe: he was condemned to perpetual imprisonment in the fortress of Ham. He received this verdict with what was now his habitual imperturbability, merely remarking: 'How long does perpetuity last in France?'

The perpetrator of two abortive coups, which had made him an object of ridicule, and now a prisoner for life, Louis Napoleon might well appear to have ruined his cause and to have reason for despair. He did indeed experience periods of deep depression during a period of imprisonment which lasted for nearly six years, but these years were also a time of forced leisure when he had ample time for reading, writing and reflection. It was in what he humorously called his 'University' of Ham that he completed his self-education, continued his propaganda and fitted himself more fully for the responsibilities of power should they ever fall upon him. Here in prison he showed that he could profit from the early training of Le Bas, set himself a strict routine, and embark upon an ambitious programme of literary work, mingled with scientific experiments. He was full of projects: the future imperial author of a *Vie de César* began to plan a life of Charlemagne. He worked upon a continuation of his *Manuel d'Artillerie*. He wrote a study of the English Revolution of 1688 (*Fragments historiques 1688 et 1830*), which had been so much in the minds of Frenchmen in 1830, and he published a pamphlet on the sugar beet industry. Moreover, as time went on, the authorities became remarkably lenient. Sensual as ever, a trait which he is thought to have inherited from Creole ancestors on the Beauharnais side, he charmed them into permitting feminine visitors, who were to bear him illegitimate children. He was able to receive other visitors, too, of a more intellectual kind such as Louis Blanc, the well-known Socialist author of *L'Organisation du Travail*. He was allowed to publish articles in provincial papers, such as the Republican *Progrès du Pas de Calais*, in which he did not scruple to stigmatize the narrowness, corruption, and lack of glory of the Orleanist regime. Finally, he brought out in 1844 a little brochure entitled *L'Extinction du Paupérisme*, the fruit of his new interest in social questions, which, he rightly hoped, would do him much good. Many of its ideas were Utopian, but it brought him fresh publicity, alarmed some conservatives and made many more of the workers aware that here was a Prince who was concerned for their lot and that this Prince was a Bonaparte, Napoleon's heir. The Government, as one historian has remarked, treated the prisoner of Ham with the tolerance that might be accorded to a naughty schoolboy. They, too, like so many others, under-estimated his power.

In a fit of exasperation at not being permitted to leave his prison on parole to visit his ailing father in Florence without undertaking to renounce all political activity, the Prince declared that he would leave Ham only for the royal palace of the Tuileries in Paris or the grave. But in May 1846 prison repairs provided an unexpected opportunity for escape, and escape he did. Two days after quitting the fortress disguised as a workman he was back in London, throwing himself en-thusiastically into the social life of which he had so long been deprived. Among the many new connexions he now formed one was to prove particularly valuable. The twenty-four year old actress Elizabeth Ann Haryett (better known as Miss Howard) was not only beautiful and became his mistress, but also wealthy and willing to place her fortune at his disposal when, in dire need of funds, he wished to exploit to the full the next great opportunity which presented itself. This opportunity, which arose in 1848, was to take him not to the Tuileries as Emperor of the French, but to the Elysée as President of the Second French Republic. But, once in the Elysée, it would be only a matter of time for the nephew of the Emperor to make his way to the Tuileries.

Chapter Two

President of the Second Republic

LOUIS NAPOLEON'S election as President of the Second Republic in December 1848 was an astonishing climax to one of the most dramatic and tragic years in modern French history. An understanding of the circumstances in which it came about and which enabled him, once in office, to consolidate his power and make himself master of the Republic, is essential to the understanding of the Second Empire.

The July Monarchy was the second French regime to fall since 1815. The Bourbons had been swept away because Charles X had violated the constitutional Charter of 1814 which had been the basis of the Restoration. Instead of gradually broadening the basis of government within the constitutional framework, he had fatally sought to narrow it in the interests of the aristocracy and the Church which were not strong enough to sustain him. In consequence, with his fall, the aristocracy, never fully reinstated in their eighteenth century power, were permanently weakened and the Church was temporarily discredited. Furthermore, the cause of monarchy itself was impaired because the breach between the families of Bourbon and Orléans, which occurred when Louis Philippe had accepted the crown in 1830, meant that the Royalists in France were henceforth divided. The July Monarchy, in turn, fell because the basis of its power was too narrow and it had refused to broaden it. Its advent had been a triumph of liberalism over reaction and of the upper bourgeoisie, the wealthy commercial and industrial interests, over the predominantly landed aristocracy. The Charter had been maintained and widened and another eighteen years of constitutional practice had enabled parliamentary habits to become well established. But the government had ignored the grave social problems arising from rapid industrialization in certain areas, their foreign policy had been prudent, but increasingly conservative, and had won them no prestige, and from the mid-'forties they had been faced by an acute economic depression which affected all Northern and Western Europe and brought widespread distress and unemployment in its train. When, despite repeated demands, they had still refused to extend the franchise, they seemed to have degenerated into a corrupt oligarchy of rich men and politicians whose only concern was to preserve their rule. In consequence, not only had they failed to rally Bonapartists, Republicans, and Legitimists, as the followers of the exiled Bourbons were called, but they had, when the final crisis came, lost the support of the lower middle classes, who had at first been among their staunchest adherents. The time had arrived for the Republicans, who had been cheated of success in 1830, to try their hand at governing France.

The First Republic had existed in name for nearly twelve years, but in fact its tumultuous existence had been brought to an end by Napoleon's *coup d'état* of Brumaire after only seven years, and already, long before 1799, it had lost much of its Republican spirit. What chances were there for the Second Republic to endure? The four months which followed the revolution of February 1848 were still more disorderly than the period following on the July Revolution of 1830. Revolution and the very name of a Republic, with its memories of terror and war, had frightened the well-to-do and caused a sharp deterioration in the already grave economic situation and a great increase in unemployment. On the other hand, for the lower classes, particularly in Paris and the big cities, the advent of a Republic seemed to be the dawn of a new era of political liberty and social reform. The old restrictions on freedom of the press and meeting were removed, a commission was set up to examine labour problems, and the franchise was extended by a decree of March 5 to all male Frenchmen of twenty years and over: the electorate was suddenly increased from about 250,000 to some 9,000,000. Moreover, the revolution made in Paris was accepted without opposition throughout the country: there was no Orleanist resistance, no Legitimist insurrection, and the new regime had the blessing of the Church which had regained vigour since 1830 and had little cause for gratitude to the July Monarchy.

Yet this new regime suffered from grave weaknesses. Not only were its leaders inexperienced men faced with internal and foreign problems of extraordinary difficulty, but they were themselves divided between democrats and socialists; they were the leaders of a party whose strength lay in the towns, but who as yet had little or no influence in the country, and they were constantly subject to the untimely pressures of Parisian demonstrators. The very freedoms which they had so liberally accorded were to make for instability and to encourage new tensions, of which an astute Pretender was to take full advantage. The Second Republic indeed started with a capital of good will and enthusiasm that progressively ebbed away, so that it has been aptly said that it 'reached its culmination at its commencement'.

Although Persigny, writing from France in mid-February 1848, had foretold that revolution was imminent, Louis Napoleon in his English exile, like many others even in France, was taken by surprise when the event occurred. But he at once recognized its significance. 'Marie', he said to a cousin, 'the Republic is proclaimed. It is for me to be its master.' His cousin smiled and told him that he was dreaming as usual. But this time the dream came true.

He had long courted Republicans and counted some like Hortense Cornu, his goddaughter and former playmate, and Vieillard, his brother's former tutor, among his closest friends. Now, if he were to master the new regime, it must be from within, in the guise of a Republican citizen. This time there would be no rash assaults from without, no hint of working for the restoration of the Empire, and Persigny would be sharply reprimanded for publicly comparing his master with Octavius. Nothing was more striking than the contrast between the rash adventurer of 1836 and 1840 and the prudent self-effacing 'man of order' of 1848.

On the morrow of the revolution he had hurried over to Paris, risking arrest, for he was still an outlaw, and for a second time offered his services to a new regime. The Provisional Government, however, headed by Lamartine, one of the Repub-

licans most impervious to his appeal and most critical of his
uncle, was beset by many thorny problems and had no wish
to be embarrassed by the presence of the Bonapartist Pretender,
loyal as his professions might be. The Prince was politely but
firmly requested to leave, and at once complied. He did so,
withdrawing, he significantly said, 'for the moment', and believing that the government would see in this 'sacrifice' the 'purity
of his intentions and of his patriotism'. This, too, was a part
he had played before. Had he not similarly 'sacrificed' himself
by withdrawing from Switzerland to England in 1837? On
March 2 he was back in England, and a month later he was
doing duty in London as one of the special constables enrolled
to face the threatened Chartist disturbances. This in itself was
a quiet but significant indication that Louis Napoleon was a
'man of order'. In the meantime, he had firmly rejected Persigny's impetuous suggestion that he should defy the ban, return
to France and head an insurrection. Had he been carried in
triumph by the National Guard to the Hôtel de Ville, he would
not, he said, have remained there for eight days. The situation
in March, so soon after the revolution, was altogether too unstable. The people, he reported, were drunk with victory and
hope. They would have to lose all their illusions before 'a
man of order could appear'. Either the Republic would be
consolidated, in which case there would be no reason for it to
prevent his return as a citizen, or it would give birth to troubles
which would be long and bloody; 'and in that case I shall plant
my name where there is opportunity for a cause that is clear
and splendid to triumph'.

Three of the most important events in the early history of
the Second Republic played into his hands, the introduction
of universal suffrage, the June Days, and the making of a new
constitution.

Universal suffrage had introduced a crucial new factor into
the situation. It meant that the 'people' or 'the masses' suddenly assumed an electoral importance such as they had not
enjoyed since the great revolution. Louis Napoleon had been
among the numerous critics of the restricted franchise of the
July Monarchy, and in his political writings had often emphasized the significance of 'the masses'. He knew very well

that the Napoleonic heritage would go, as the *Constitutionnel* had predicted, to the man who knew how to rally these masses. 'What would in their eyes eternally distinguish Napoleon from other sovereigns', he had told Lamartine in 1843, was that he was 'the king of the people, while the others were the kings of the nobles and privileged'. 'To-day', he had written in *L'Extinction du Paupérisme*, 'the reign of castes is ended: one can govern only with the masses; they must therefore be organized so that they can formulate their wishes and disciplined so that they may be directed and enlightened concerning their own interests'. (Later he expressed the same idea more cynically: 'the nation is a slave who must be made to believe that she is on the throne'.) The significance of universal suffrage and the opportunities it presented were thus at once apparent to him. Years earlier, Chateaubriand had advised him that the only way to overthrow Louis Philippe was to become eligible as a deputy, win an election, attempt by his talent to gain a majority in the Chamber, and then make use of his power to dethrone the King and take his place. Whether or not he remembered the great writer's counsel, this was approximately the course he was slowly and patiently to follow in a different regime.

But he was in no haste to become a deputy, and refused to stand as a candidate when the new electorate first went to the polls in the general elections in April 1848. An organization had yet to be created and money to be found, if the image of the Emperor's nephew were to be triumphantly projected on the Republican screen; for, on the morrow of the revolution, when Republican papers and clubs abounded, there was no Bonapartist club of any moment and no press except one ephemeral newspaper and an expiring review; nor was there any organization, only a small group of faithful adherents, some of whom had been with Louis Napoleon at Strasbourg and Boulogne, and, up and down the country, many who were emotionally loyal to the memory of the Emperor. All this was gradually remedied. All available funds were mobilized—significantly two of the Prince's chief financial backers were women, his cousin Princess Mathilde and Miss Howard, who is said to have contributed £80,000—and his supporters went to work with a will, multiplied, and set up a committee which embarked on a great campaign of publicity. His name and features were made known in portraits—some punningly entitled simply 'Lui'—on medals and matchboxes and flags, in the chanting of 'Poléon nous l'aurons', and in a multitude of other ways calculated to appeal to the mass of still largely illiterate voters.

Meanwhile, the result of the April elections had been encouraging to Bonapartists and Conservatives and discomfiting to the Republicans. Two Bonaparte princes and a Murat had been returned, and the peasantry, often guided by the clergy, had shown their distrust of the Parisian extremists by electing to the Constituent Assembly a large majority of conservatives, who had stood as Republicans, but many of whom were Legitimists or Orleanists at heart. The tension between the capital and the countryside in consequence grew more severe.

The system of multiple elections which now operated was also to be to Louis Napoleon's advantage, as later on it carried Thiers to the chief magistracy of the Third Republic in 1871 and General Boulanger to the brink of dictatorship in 1887. It meant that a would-be deputy could stand and be elected at the same time in several different constituencies, choosing after the elections which one he would represent. It meant that in May 1848 a number of supplementary or by-elections had to be held and that in them Louis Napoleon was returned for Paris and three departments. But he had still not wished to stand—indeed his candidature had been put forward by his henchmen in France against his express wishes. He was convinced that the time was not yet ripe for him to go back to France—his name and antecedents, he told Vieillard, made of him for good or for ill not a party leader but a man to whom all the discontented were looking—and he feared that his presence would serve as a pretext for disorder in a capital still subject to constant demonstrations. So, gratified though he was by his election, he hesitated to take his seat and, when he learnt that incidents had occurred which had induced the government to imprison two of his chief agents, Persigny and Laity, and to order his own arrest should he set foot in France, he promptly wrote to the President of the Assembly a letter of resignation, reaffirming his desire for order and the maintenance of 'a wise, great and intelligent Republic'.

His prudence was quickly and amply justified. A few days later the Parisian workers were driven to insurrection by the decision of the Constituent Assembly with its conservative majority to close the National Workshops which had been set up to relieve unemployment. This rising of the June Days and its harsh repression cruelly ended the honeymoon period of popular illusions. The trouble Louis Napoleon had foreseen for the Republic had ended in bloodshed and a Republican government had had to call in a general, Cavaignac, to take over power and crush Republican workers.

The Prince's supporters accordingly redoubled their propaganda—it was from June onwards that the number of Bonapartist newspapers significantly increased. Louis Napoleon could now begin deliberately to 'plant' his name and work for the triumph of 'a clear and splendid cause'. When still further elections were to be held in September he consented to stand, and did so as one of those candidates who could 'help public reconciliation'. His programme was astute and revealing. 'There is one name which is a symbol of order, of glory and of patriotism. The man who bears it to-day has won the confidence and affection of the people . . . let his name be a first pledge of reconciliation. He will obtain an amnesty for the unfortunate men condemned in June and his knowledge of political and social questions will help him to save you from unemployment, poverty, and anarchy'. This time he was elected again in Paris and by four other departments. Significantly, in Paris he headed the list and defeated the nominee of General Cavaignac, who was to be his chief rival for the presidency. Significantly, too, the man who stood for reconciliation and for order and economic betterment could be returned both by the capital and by rural areas. It was after this quintuple election, a minor plebiscite as some historians have called it, that Victor Hugo wrote his famous comment in *L'Evénement*: 'Since 1815 the people have been waiting for Napoleon . . . The man whom the people has just named as its representative is not the heir of the skirmish at Boulogne, he is the victor of June . . . His candidature dates from Austerlitz'. The man who became a deputy under such auspices might well aspire to higher things. But would the constitution make their achievement possible?

'As long as the constitution is unsettled', Louis Napoleon had written in May, 'I feel that my position in France will be very difficult, very embarrassing and even very dangerous.' So, even after the June days, he had resolutely stayed on in his English exile. But by the beginning of September the draft of the new constitution was known and it included the proposal that the President of the Republic, as well as the legislature, should be elected by universal suffrage. Here was an opportunity indeed for the man who had just been returned by five constituencies and who, in a disquieting phrase in his letter of June 14 to the President of the Assembly, had said that if the people 'were to impose duties' upon him he would 'know how to fulfil them'. It was time for the new deputy to take his seat and make himself personally known to his countrymen. When he reached Paris the Assembly had begun to debate the constitution: and for him the immediately crucial question was whether it would accept or reject the proposals concerning the Presidency. There were many speakers, including a future President of the Third Republic, Jules Grévy, who, fearing that direct popular election would lead to dictatorship, urged that the Assembly itself should make the choice. Had they won the day, Louis Napoleon would have had no chance of being elected, at least in 1848, for his strength lay with the people not with the politicians, and the history of the Second Republic would have been very different. But at this juncture good fortune intervened in the person of Lamartine. For all his distrust of the Prince—he had said that all the harm done by the uncle would be multiplied a hundredfold by the nephew . . . 'after the ogre, the little ogre'—Lamartine was a man of principle, with a doctrinaire belief in direct popular sovereignty, and his eloquent but ill-judged speech, ending with the cry that something must be left to Providence, swung his colleagues into supporting the motion by a large majority. One great obstacle was removed. There was, however, another to be overcome. Could a member of an ex-ruling house be eligible? The debate on this issue caused Louis Napoleon to intervene in his own defence, but he was no more at home in a stormy Chamber than his famous uncle had been at Saint Cloud in 1799, faltered, and was unable to finish his speech. His humiliation, surprisingly, was his salvation. The deputy who had introduced the ineligibility motion withdrew it, remarking that after what the Assembly had just seen and heard, it was no longer necessary. Two days later the law banishing the Bonapartes was abrogated.

The constitution as a whole was approved by the Assembly on November 4 and the presidential election was due to be held on December 10. The Prince accepted candidature because, he said, 'three successive elections and the unanimous decree of the Assembly against the proscription of my family authorise me to believe that France regards my name as able to serve the consolidation of society'. Consolidation—this was what the people wanted—consolidation and reassurance after months of fear: the country people wanted reassurance that their property would not be taken from them by Parisian Republicans and that they would not be subjected to yet further increases in direct taxation; the bourgeoisie would support the man whose prestige might help to restore confidence in the economy; the workers would vote for the author of *L'Extinction du Paupérisme* rather than for his chief rival, General Cavaignac, who had suppressed the June rising; the Church was disposed to support the candidate who had declared his readiness to maintain the temporal sovereignty of the Pope and to secure freedom of education at home; and the army could be counted on to back a Bonaparte who had constantly reiterated his concern for their glory and well-being. All this movement of support was given momentum by the skilful propaganda of the Prince's election agents and strengthened by the personal relations he had established with the principal conservative politicians. As early as March he had observed that it was now in the interests of 'the rich and monarchist class' to show him sympathy, and in July he had written that the great thing would be to have the support of 'men of government' and intelligence such as Thiers, one of the leading politicians of the Orleanist regime. Now, divided among themselves, with no obvious agreed candidate of their own willing to stand against Louis Napoleon, these men too, Thiers, Molé, Montalembert and others, along with the most influential journalists of the day, decided, *faute de mieux*, to throw their weight behind the candidate whose name was so likely to ensure success and who so resolutely declared himself a man of order. Perhaps, too, they consoled themselves with the belief that they could make him their tool and that he would be a useful stopgap until they achieved their own Restoration, not of Empire, but of Monarchy.

They were indeed right in believing that nothing succeeds like success. The result of the election was an overwhelming triumph, 'not', as Girardin said, 'an election, but an acclamation' of Louis Napoleon. He was returned with nearly five and a half million votes, compared with nearly one and a half given to Cavaignac and less than half a million distributed among other Republican candidates, including Lamartine. 'The man of order' had been returned, a candidate of the Right rather than of the Left, but above all the chosen of the new electorate, of 'the masses' and especially of the peasantry, who throughout would be his most solid support.

This result was a remarkable posthumous triumph, twenty-seven years after his death at St. Helena, for the Emperor, whose cult could flourish, and had done so, independently of 'the legend'. We shall never know precisely how much the 'legend' counted in this triumph, but there is little doubt that Persigny was right when he had written in November that the name of Napoleon was a political force which rested much more upon a sentiment than on ideas, and that Félix Pyat summed up the reasons for Louis Napoleon's election as well as anyone when he wrote: 'There was a little of everything in this vote; men voted for the insurrectionist of Strasbourg and for the Socialist author, but above all for the nephew of the Emperor. Above all, the people wanted the nephew to continue the work of his uncle, that is to say the Revolution . . . the Empire was part of the Revolution . . . it was the principle of equality opposed to the principle of heredity, the idea of progress opposed to the idea of conservation, individual right opposed to the privilege of birth and caste'. That was what the people wanted. Louis Napoleon in a sense appeared as the first of the supposed supermen in whom 'the masses' sought to find the personification of their own confused aspirations. But with his election, as Victor Hugo said, 'the future entered on the stage, a future unknown'. For all his published programmes, the Emperor's nephew would be to his contemporaries a baffling and unpredictable character; and, paradoxically, during his reign of apparent stability France was to live more dangerously than in times of much greater disorder.

Until ten weeks before his election as President, Louis Napoleon since the age of seven had set foot in France only as a refugee, a conspirator, a prisoner, or an outlaw. Until he took his seat as deputy few of the nine hundred members of the Constituent Assembly had ever set eyes on him. When they did so, few were impressed by this man of five foot five, with legs short in proportion to his body, rounded back, head sunk between broad shoulders, brown moustache, small 'imperial' beard, large nose, and expressionless grey eyes. When they also remarked his reserve and apparent timidity and noted his indifference as a speaker many, who equated oratory with political talent, dismissed him as a nonentity, 'a melancholy parrot', in General Changarnier's phrase. But others who came to know him better saw that he had been underrated. He was far from handsome but he had a powerful head, a simplicity and dignity of bearing, and an aristocratic perfection of manners which well became a chief of state. He had physical courage to a high degree and looked at his best on horseback. He was, moreover, kind and generous and possessed an extraordinary indefinable charm, which, when they met him face to face, powerfully attracted many even of those who had been most prejudiced against him. This was a great political asset, but it was offset by what one historian has called 'the most complete and ingenuous lack of moral sense', for this lack was to be as evident in his public as in his private life. As for his capacity for statesmanship, this was an unknown quantity. It was one thing to be a superb tactician in the direction of propaganda and the conduct of an election campaign, but how would this 'dreamer' cope with the daily routine and the complexities of rule in a country so difficult to govern as France?

It has been suggested that on the morrow of his election Louis Napoleon lost a great opportunity by not following Persigny's advice and refusing to take the oath unless the constitution was first submitted to popular approval. Such a step, it has been argued, would have placed him in a position so strong that he could have speedily restored the Empire without any of the difficulties he subsequently encountered. Had he thus ridden the crest of the December wave of popular enthusiasm he might have succeeded, but it would have been a great gamble for a man who as yet knew France so little at first hand and had none of his assured supporters in key positions. As the British Ambassador wrote: 'the President finds himself suddenly at the head of a country of which he has no practical knowledge, without a single personal friend of any political standing, with ill-defined functions and divided responsibility.' He needed time to feel his way, to size up the politicians, to learn the arts of government. Moreover, he was both a man who, having won a success, preferred for a while to avoid further risks, and an opportunist who might well think that with four years ahead he would have leisure to prepare for the achievement of his supreme ambition. Meanwhile, he could test the strength of parties, allow them partly to devour one another, try out the policies which he wished to make his own, and form his own group of 'men of the Elysée', who in due course would help him to found and govern the Empire.

His first year of office was in any case a test. France was still suffering from economic depression and the after-effects of revolution and civil war, while the greater part of Europe was painfully returning to a state of order imposed from above by force of arms. The Constituent Assembly in its last months was increasingly unmanageable and the elections in the spring of 1849 to the first parliament under the new constitution, the Legislative Assembly, while completing the discomfiture of the moderate Republicans, showed a disquieting tendency for opinion to coalesce about the extremes. On the one hand the Catholics and Royalists, the 'Party of Order', increased their vote by 30 per cent, on the other the democrats or men of the Mountain returned 180 strong, thus sharpening the prevailing conservative fear of a 'Red' Republic. In the midst of all this the President had to work a new and untried constitution. His ministers, for the most part conservative politicians, were men whom he scarcely knew and who sought to ignore him. He was confronted by difficult questions of foreign policy, especially in Italy, and by outbreaks of disorder culminating in a fresh attempt at insurrection in Paris in 1849.

The Prince President, as he was now generally called, faced these difficulties for the most part with consummate skill. He quickly made it clear that he would not be a mere 'prisoner' in the Elysée or play the part of decorative figurehead that Sieyès in 1800 had vainly designed for Napoleon. He insisted not only on wearing uniform and establishing a military household, but on being consulted by his ministers, and although he did not succeed in his demand to see the files on his Strasbourg and Boulogne adventures, the demand forced a minor ministerial reconstruction. 'Man of order', he successfully backed the ministers against the Constituent Assembly which sought unduly to prolong its existence, but he refused to yield to suggestions that he should dissolve it by force. He fulfilled his pledges to the Roman Catholics by supporting the principle of freedom of education which was to result in the Loi Falloux of March 1850 and by countenancing the restoration of Papal Government at Rome in 1849. This ensured him the continued support of the powerful Catholic interests. But the Roman question did more than this. Although it landed him in a dilemma abroad, it enabled him still further to strengthen his authority at home.

It was a strange chance indeed that the Papal States, where he had made his own adventurous début in politics eighteen years earlier, should set him his first difficult problem in foreign policy. Italy, too, had been thrown into turmoil in 1848 and a wave of nationalist feeling had carried all except the Papal States into war against Austria. At the end of the year, menaced by Republicans and nationalists in his own dominions, Pope Pius IX had fled to Gaeta in Neapolitan territory, and early in 1849 a Republic was set up in Rome. Soon afterwards Austria defeated Piedmont for a second time and regained the upper hand in Northern Italy. It looked as though her next move might be to intervene in Rome and crush the Roman Republic.

It was, however, an established principle of French policy not to allow the whole of Italy to be dominated from Vienna, and in authorizing the despatch of an expedition to Rome to forestall Austria Louis Napoleon and his ministers, who had already guaranteed the integrity of Piedmont, were maintaining the balance of power in the peninsula and following a pattern of counter-intervention already traced under the July Monarchy. But the French government's attitude towards the Roman Republic was equivocal. They had spoken of reconciling the Pope to his subjects, yet no indication was given how this was to be done or whether the expedition was intended to overthrow or maintain the Republic. What Louis Napoleon himself intended we do not certainly know. No doubt he believed that the French would be welcomed in Rome as its defenders against Austria and hoped that the subject of the city's future government might then be a matter for negotiation in such a way that he could redeem his pledge to French Catholics without alienating Italian Liberals. But, when the French had unexpectedly been denied entry to Rome by Garibaldi's men and repulsed beneath the walls, he ordered up reinforcements to redress the humiliation. An agreement concluded by the special French envoy with Mazzini, whereby the Roman Republic accepted French protection, was repudiated, since de Lesseps had exceeded his instructions, and on June 3 General Oudinot began the siege of the city.

When this news reached Paris the Republicans in the Legislative Assembly were furious. They denounced both the ministers and the Prince-President for violating Article 5 of the constitution, which stated that the Republic should never use its forces against the liberties of any people. They demanded that they should be brought to trial, and they went on to threaten insurrection. The rising that followed on June 13 was a fiasco, for the workers of Paris had had enough of barricades and would not follow their bourgeois leaders. It gave the Prince-President, however, a new opportunity to display his personal courage by riding about the streets of Paris with only a small entourage and to reiterate his role as 'man of order'; a resounding proclamation contained a famous phrase: 'It is time for the good to be reassured and for the wicked to tremble'.

Three weeks later the French entry into Rome meant the overthrow of the Republic there. The humiliation of the spring had been avenged, but Louis Napoleon had reckoned without the Pope and was soon to be baffled by Papal obstruction. The duel between Napoleon I and Pius VII had been a conspicuous theme of the First Empire. There now began the long duel between Louis Napoleon and Pius IX over the Roman question which was to bedevil the Second Empire. The French established a garrison in Rome to prepare the way for the Pope's return. But Pius IX was no longer the liberal he had appeared to be in 1846–8. He allowed a Commission of Cardinals to embark on a policy of reaction and refused to listen to French representations that he should modify it. Louis Napoleon, who had not fought in 1831 to preserve Papal despotism, was no doubt genuinely angry, but he adroitly exploited the unwelcome development to enhance his authority at home. He made his displeasure known in a personal letter on August 18 to his A.D.C., Colonel Edgar Ney, which was at once made public. The French Republic, he said, had not sent an army to Rome to stifle Italian liberty, but to regulate it and give it a solid basis. This, in his view, entailed a general amnesty, secularisation of the administration, the Code Napoléon and liberal government. The letter worsened his relations both with the Pope, who now refused to return to Rome, and with his ministers. But this deterioration at home was his opportunity. When, in subsequent debates, the ministers affected to ignore the letter to Ney, Louis Napoleon dismissed them, despite the fact that they had not lost their parliamentary support. In a message on October 31, justifying his action, he complained of a lack of unity and of a confusion which was troubling France and causing her to grope for the guiding 'hand and will of the man elected on December 10'. 'A whole system' had triumphed on December 10, for the name of Napoleon was 'in itself a whole programme'. That programme must be maintained and the country saved, 'in spite of the parties, ambitions, and even imperfections which our constitution may contain'. The dismissal was, as a French historian has remarked, virtually 'a little *coup d'état*', which struck a blow at the parliamentary regime from which it was not for years to recover. Thenceforward the Prince-President could make and unmake ministers much as he pleased. Thereby he obtained an indispensable control over key personnel in the final struggle with the legislature which gave him mastery of France. His new cabinet included names of two men little known at the time, who would, however, become his leading ministers on and off during the next ten to twenty years, Achille Fould, a banker, and Eugène Rouher, an able lawyer, not yet 35. Others soon followed, notably Baroche, who became Minister of the Interior in 1850.

To the achievement of his ultimate aim of restoring the Empire there were three main obstacles, the hostility of the Republicans, many of whom now identified him with the party of order and repression, the opposition of the Monarchists who, when they saw that he would not restore the monarchy for them, planned to do it for themselves, and 'the imperfections' of the constitution, to which he had alluded on October 31, in particular the provision that the President of the Republic at the end of his four years' term of office could not immediately be re-elected.

The Republicans, however, had been successively cowed. Many of their leaders had been driven into exile in 1848 and 1849, and the Assembly had done much of Louis Napoleon's work for him by the repressive legislation they had put through after the rising of June 1849 and after the new 'Red' scare caused by the successes of the Mountain in the complementary elections in the spring of 1850. The Monarchists were thereafter more dangerous, because of their majority in the Chamber, because after the death of Louis Philippe in April 1850 the chances increased that they would end the Orleanist-Legitimist feud and present a united front, and because one of their men, General Changarnier, combined the key posts of Commander of the National Guard and of the Paris garrison. But the negotiations for Monarchist 'fusion', 'the union of foolscap and blotting-paper' as it was called by Walter Savage Landor, came to nought. Accordingly, in January 1851 Louis Napoleon felt strong enough to brave the wrath of the Assembly and, seizing on a dispute over military discipline, made it the pretext for dismissing Changarnier.

There remained the third obstacle, which could legally be surmounted only by constitutional revision. Unfortunately for Louis Napoleon, the authors of the constitution, like many other constitution-makers proud of their work, had contrived that this should be a highly difficult operation. It could not be embarked upon before the Assembly had entered upon its last year, and then only after the deputies in three successive debates at monthly intervals had, by a three-quarter's majority of the votes cast, registered their desire for change.

Thus the year 1851–2 would be a crucial one, and there were many who, because of these obstacles in the way of Louis Napoleon's maintenance in power, had seen the shadow of a *coup d'état* darkening the future of the Second Republic almost from the morrow of his election to the Presidency. Already in February 1850 Fortoul, one of the 'familiars' of the Elysée, could prophesy that 'one fine morning a picket of soldiers will forbid us entry to the Assembly and a Constitution coming from above [i.e. from the Prince-President] will be proposed not to the Chamber but to the country. The electoral system will be profoundly modified. Probably, the representative regime will be suspended. A Senate and a Council of State appointed by the executive will take care of things provisionally. At the first demonstration of this kind the whole of France will applaud. Even the Legitimists will be divided. The army will do the rest'. This very interesting passage from Fortoul's correspondence suggests that Louis Napoleon and his intimates had already sketched the outlines of a possible coup more than eighteen months before it took place. But there is no doubt that he had no wish to employ force, if it could possibly be avoided, and that he wanted to do his utmost to secure the constitutional revision which would have permitted his re-election by another massive popular vote. Thereafter the peaceful transition from Republic to Empire might be effected as easily as in 1804.

In the struggles which dominated the year 1851 Louis Napoleon again showed himself a masterly player of political chess, reinforcing his own position in the country and discrediting that of the Assembly. The constitutional arrangements had the further defect of causing the terms of President

and Assembly to expire almost simultaneously in the spring of
1852. Thus there was a great opportunity for Louis Napoleon
and his adherents to stress the critical situation in which the
country might find itself, to revive the 'Red' spectre, and to
conjure up a picture of left-wing insurrection and renewed
anarchy, should it be left without a government or any con-
stituted authority. This was a telling argument with those who
had suffered in 1848 but, by 1850, were beginning to reap the
benefits of returning economic prosperity. From the first, moreover, Louis Napoleon had sought to strengthen his position by
using his powers of appointment, by developing a personal
following, by cultivating the army and by making himself
known to the provinces. In his provincial tours—in August
1850 he visited over fifty towns—he delivered a series of brief
but often felicitous and adroit addresses, in which he frequently reminded his hearers that he, 'the man elected by six
million votes', was their representative as much as the Assembly
and that, if the country was not yet as prosperous as it should
be, this was due to the way in which his efforts were impeded
by factions and manoeuvres. These tactics bore fruit. Already
in 1850 a majority of general councils had expressed desire
for constitutional revision. In 1851 a vigorous campaign by his
supporters provoked petitions in favour of revision from all
over the country. But their efforts were vain. The opposition
of Republicans, of Thiers and his friends (who hoped that
Thiers would be elected President in 1852), and of a number of
die-hard Legitimists prevented the motion for revision from
obtaining the necessary majority when the question came up for
debate in July. Louis Napoleon was faced with the alternatives
of retiring into private life or maintaining himself in power
by means of a *coup d'état*.

A *coup d'état* he had seemingly long though reluctantly envisaged, despite his oath and despite the fact that the constitution laid down that, if the President made any attempt to
dissolve the Legislature or prevent it from fulfilling its mandate, he would be deemed to have committed high treason
and automatically be deposed. His half-brother, Morny, had
told a correspondent in February 1851 that he did not think
revision would obtain the necessary majority and that, if it

failed, 'the Assembly will find itself so unpopular that it will have to disappear—followed by the curses of the country. But in any case it must have a violent ending'. Louis Napoleon was to ensure that the unpopularity of the Assembly was still further increased, Morny himself to play a major part in ensuring the violent ending.

One of the most unpopular of the Assembly's reactionary measures, following upon Republican victories in complementary elections held in the spring of 1850, had been the law of May 31 which had the effect of disfranchising nearly three million people. Now, in the autumn of 1851, the Prince-President adroitly made a bid to recover the support of the democrats by proposing the repeal of this law. When this proposal was rejected in November by a small majority the Assembly could still more easily be made to appear a body of narrow and reactionary politicians who constantly frustrated his generous intentions and by refusing revision threatened to plunge the country again into civil war. 'How great France could be,' declared Louis Napoleon in a speech in November 1851, 'if she were permitted to attend to her real business, and reform her institutions instead of being incessantly troubled either by demagogic ideas or by Monarchist hallucinations!'.

By now everyone expected the coup that soon occurred. The Assembly, unable, like the Convention earlier, even to organize its own defence, waited, paralysed yet fascinated, like the Ancients and the Five Hundred in 1797, for the blow to fall. Meanwhile Louis Napoleon had made his plans with meticulous care. Those on whom he could rely, tough careerists, 'brutal adventurers' one historian has called them, Saint-Arnaud, Magnan, Morny, and Maupas had been or were to be placed in the key posts of Commander of the Paris garrison, Minister of War, Minister of the Interior and Prefect of Police. After many postponements, the day chosen for 'operation Rubicon' was December 2, the anniversary of Austerlitz. That had been regarded by Napoleon I as his lucky day. The choice was characteristic of his nephew who also believed in his own star. In the very early morning, what Morny euphemistically described as 'a slightly rough police operation' began. Troops were massed in key positions, a number of leading deputies and

others, including Thiers and Generals Cavaignac, Changarnier
and Lamoricière, nearly 80 persons in all, were arrested and
the parliament house, the Palais Bourbon, was occupied. Opposition newspapers were seized and new decrees and proclamations, secretly printed, were posted in public places. All these
operations were completed by 8 a.m. Three hundred deputies
who later attempted to form a committee of resistance were
easily dispersed.

The coup was brilliantly executed and possibly forestalled
an Orleanist plan to put the Prince de Joinville in power. But
it was not, like Brumaire, to be bloodless. The reaction of the
city as a whole was as yet uncertain. Morny was prepared, if
resistance were shown, to let it develop and then to crush it
once and for all. So, when a few barricades did go up on the
3rd in one or two quarters, the troops dealt roughly with those
who opposed them, and unhappily on the 4th incidents on the
Boulevard de la Poissonnière provoked them to fire indis-
criminately, causing some two or three hundred casualties,
including many bystanders. Paris was effectively cowed, but at
a price which cost the Prince-President dear. In the provinces
too, in certain regions of the Centre and South, where the
Republicans had succeeded in extending their hold, there was
resistance which was enough to provide the authors of the
coup with the pretext for draconian repression, harsher still
than that which had followed the June Days. Some 27,000
persons were arrested and, though many were released, 9,000
were deported to Algeria.

Meanwhile Louis Napoleon had issued proclamations justifying his action, calling on the people to ratify it, and
indicating the outlines of a new constitution. The plebiscite
which followed was an overwhelming endorsement of the *coup
d'état* and of the new order. Seven and a half million voters
registered their approval and only half a million dissented.
Even allowing for official pressure it was clear that France
had no regrets for the Assembly and was prepared to trust the
man who had overthrown it. Louis Napoleon was master of
France.

Chapter Three

The New System

THE way was now clear for the 'new era' in which France's master would remould her institutions in accordance with the views he had so often outlined and achieve at last the ambition he had cherished for so long. Although it was not proclaimed for nearly a year, the Second Empire dates in fact, if not in name, from the *coup d'état* of December 1851. Already in February 1852 Parisian society was declining the phrase 'L'empire se fait, l'empire se fera, l'empire s'est fait.'

Few regimes in modern French history have borne so strongly the imprint of a single hand, few have depended so much on the strength or vacillation of a single mind, and few have been so diversely estimated. On the one hand Louis Napoleon's new 'system' has been denounced as authoritarian and retrograde, a police state resting on the twin pillars of army and Church; on the other it has been defended as a necessary phase in France's political development, a phase marked by unparalleled economic progress and notable social improvements. On the one hand its progenitor has been condemned as a muddled dreamer, in whose reign France 'lost the leadership of Europe in politics, in economics, and in culture'; on the other he has been hailed as a man who understood the fundamental problems of his day better than any ruler of his time, 'a better European than Bismarck or Gambetta and a better socialist than Karl Marx'. This variety of judgment and the inscrutability of the Prince-President (who after the *coup d'état* was no longer being called by his critics 'an imbecile' but 'a sphinx') and of the Emperor who confided in so few and committed so little to paper make all the more fascinating the study of a ruler and a regime whose vicissitudes were profoundly to affect both the fortunes of France and the whole balance of European power.

Louis Napoleon constructed the framework of his new 'system' with such remarkable rapidity and determination that it was virtually complete within a few months of the *coup d'état*. Its structure was in sharp and calculated contrast to those of the preceding regimes since 1815. Where they had been liberal, it was authoritarian. Where they had had a limited franchise, it was based on a restored universal suffrage. Where they had separated the powers of legislature, executive and judiciary, it contrived that a dominant executive should trench upon and subordinate the other two. Where they had been parliamentary, it was representative but anti-parliamentary. Where they had borrowed from Anglo-Saxon models, it was, so Louis Napoleon claimed, 'entirely French', a system which had already been tried half a century earlier and proved its worth. Indeed, the preamble to the constitution of January 14, 1852, reads like a brief summary of *Des Idées Napoléoniennes*, first published more than twelve years before. It expressed the Prince-President's 'long-formed' conviction that, since Napoleon I's administrative work, 'the framework of the edifice of our society', had outlasted his fall and three revolutions, there was no reason why his political institutions should not, if reintroduced, have the same chance of enduring. The constitution which followed was consciously modelled upon that of the Year VIII (1800), whose virtues the Emperor's nephew had so often extolled.

The outstanding feature of France's government in Louis Napoleon's 'new era' was its authoritarianism. For nearly three months until the coming into force of the new constitution at the end of March, 1852, he exercised a personal dictatorship and governed by decree, depriving political offenders of the vote, restricting the liberty of the press, dissolving the National Guard, so long a characteristic but sometimes turbulent institution in post-Revolutionary France, and appropriating the property of the Orléans family for purposes of public charity. These measures 'liquidating' the former regime were so severe that some men might well wonder whether this 'dreamer' was in reality a cruel tyrant or had not within him, as Lord Cowley later suggested, a vengeful streak. For the moment, however, taken in conjunction with the harshness and magnitude of the repression which had followed the resistance in the provinces, they too helped to emphasise, as no doubt the Prince-President intended that they should, the view that the *coup d'état* was a measure which had saved France from imminent civil war and not the act of an ambitious individual who had not scrupled to break his oath in order to maintain himself in power.

When the new constitution, the outlines of which had already been indicated in a proclamation, was promulgated, it was seen to give the Prince-President powers such as no ruler had enjoyed since Napoleon, or, as Sainte-Beuve suggested, Louis XIV. Louis Napoleon was to hold office for ten years, to nominate his successor, to have the right to appeal directly to the people whenever he wished, to command the armed forces, to declare war and conclude treaties of peace, alliance and commerce, to appoint to all public offices and to issue the necessary regulations and decrees for the execution of laws which he alone could initiate. He could declare a state of siege in one or more departments, the ministers depended on him alone and could not act as a team, and they and the members of the legislature and all public servants were required to take an oath of loyalty to him and of fidelity to the constitution.

Beside this all-powerful executive the other institutions were dwarfed indeed. The legislature, in particular, was a shadow compared with its predecessors since 1815. There were to be two houses of parliament with names revived from Napoleonic times. The upper, the Senate, was a body of nominated or *ex-officio* dignitaries, whose main function was to act as the guardians of the constitution. It was not, however, purely ornamental, for the Senators could also modify the constitution and the ruler was to have in them a convenient and pliable instrument of change. The lower house or Legislative Body was to be a modest assembly of some 260 deputies instead of the 750 of its predecessor. They were indeed, unlike the Legislative Body of the First Empire, to be elected by universal suffrage, but could meet for only three months a year and then only to discuss the bills proposed by the President and prepared and put before them by the expert body of the Council of State. They had no right to interpellate the Ministers or even to debate the annual address on the state of the nation sent to them by the President of the Republic. Their two chief officers were to be nominated by him and their proceedings could not even be reported by the press, which had to content itself with publishing the official record drawn up by the President of the Legislative Body. Thus they were virtually deprived of any power of genuine political discussion and became, as a contemporary said, a 'faceless parliament' (un parlement anonyme), which, in Louis Napoleon's words, would not waste its time 'in vain interpellations, in frivolous accusations and in passionate struggles, the only object of which was to overthrow the ministers in order to take their place'. As though to symbolise the altered status of the deputy, the orator's tribune itself was taken away and those who wished to speak now had to do so from the places in which they were sitting.

The powers of the legislature might be vastly reduced, but it was still desirable to ensure that the persons elected to it were men approved by the government, that no undue interest in politics was displayed by the public at large, and that good order continued to prevail. The central administration, so often praised by Louis Napoleon as his uncle's creation, was therefore a pivotal element in his new system. By various measures he contrived to increase its status and its *esprit de corps* with the result that, although it did not exceed 250,000 in number, it had a more thorough control of the country than at any time since Napoleon I. In particular, he enhanced the powers, salaries, and dignity of those key men in the departments, the prefects, he saw that there was greater continuity of direction in the Ministry of the Interior—between 1848 and 1851 there had been no fewer than twelve Ministers—and he trebled the numbers of the gendarmerie and increased those of the police.

It was on the Minister of the Interior, the prefects, and the mayors that the main work fell of 'guiding' the people and of ensuring that election results were satisfactory to the government. The Minister did not scruple to alter the boundaries of constituencies when this seemed expedient or to continue the time-honoured system of official pressure on behalf of candidates supported by the government. Indeed, in the first elections of 1852, Persigny who held the post from 1852 to 1854 was franker than any of his predecessors: 'The public good can be assured only on condition that the Legislative Body is in perfect harmony of ideas with the Head of the State. In consequence, M. le Préfet, by the intermediary of the various agents of the administration, and by any and every means you consider consistent with the feeling in your area . . . you should take all steps necessary to bring to the attention of the electors of your Department those candidates that the Government of Louis Napoleon judges to be most useful in helping him in his work of reconstruction.' The fact that the system of voting had been altered, the *scrutin de liste* at the chief town of the canton having been replaced by *scrutin uninominal* (designed to represent local rather than national interests) whereby electors voted for one man in their commune, facilitated such administrative pressures; while the device whereby only official candidates had the right to print notices on white paper could be a serious handicap to candidates not approved by the government. The prefects did their work well. It was only to be expected that after voting so recently in the plebiscite the people should be less interested in turning out again to vote for a Chamber so reduced in powers. There were 3½ million abstentions, but only nine of the new deputies were not government men, and, as those of them who were Republicans refused to take the oath of allegiance, the President of the Republic was secure in a Chamber which, for its term of six years, was likely to be as subservient as he could wish.

He was indeed so secure that, as has been pointed out, now was the time when 'a personal regime, served by a powerful propaganda and the omnipresent activity of a single party', could have supplanted the representative system. But Louis Napoleon was not in this respect the herald of the twentieth-century dictator. Indeed, it is a remarkable fact that the Bonapartist party, which had gradually been developed since 1848, was disbanded on the eve of the 1852 elections. The Prince-President aspired to be above parties and, this being so, a party which, apart from his immediate entourage, was largely composed of men of little standing was a doubtful asset. He aimed at conquering the men of substance and the élite of the country by the success of his policies and by judicious overtures. The concept of the monolithic party as an indispensable instrument of dictatorship, regimenting the entire life of a nation, was not yet acclimatized in Western Europe.

The other great safeguard against overmuch political excitement was the muzzling of the press. This, too, was nothing new, but Louis Napoleon's 'organic' decree of February 17, 1852, united almost all the restrictions devised since 1814 with a new and more subtle method of administrative control. The Minister of the Interior in Paris and the prefects in the provinces could give a warning to any paper which printed an article which they thought objectionable. After three warnings the offending journal was liable to suspension for two months, and any paper so suspended might be suppressed by the President of the Republic. This system was an ingenious means of placing the onus for good behaviour on the papers themselves. But the most immediately effective measure in reducing the activities of the press was the requirement that founders and publishers of newspapers must obtain government authorization. Within a few months the number of political dailies appearing in Paris was reduced to four and by 1865 the number in the provinces had been diminished from some 430 to 260.

Yet the France thus regimented was not, in spite of the power and efficacy of the central administration, a merely bureaucratic state like the Austrian Empire, for although the whole emphasis was shifted from politics to administration, the bureaux while they were powerful to obstruct, seldom positively determined policy. Even the ministers themselves, it was said, were 'in fact only the executors or technical advisers of a will of whose character they are often ignorant up to the last moment, but to which they docilely submit even when its decisions are the opposite of advice they previously gave'. That will was the will of a man who still maintained a conspiratorial taste for his own special sources of information and for his own extra-official contacts and secret interviews.

Although not a police state in the twentieth century sense, since the police were not the instruments of a single party devoted to a ruthless ideology, Louis Napoleon's France, like his uncle's, was, as a necessary corollary of his authoritarian system, kept under close supervision. The police (whose precise role is one of the obscurer aspects of the history of the Second Empire) were omnipresent and their powers and functions were extended (although there was no notable increase in secret police funds). In particular, the gendarmerie, enlarged by a ruler who had been a London special constable and admired the English police, contributed much to the improvement of public order and to the detection of crime as well as being a highly efficient instrument of surveillance. The police were not, however, a separate power apart from the Ministry of the Interior. The experiment of reviving a separate Ministry of General Police under Maupas lasted only eighteen months and was then ended because of the opposition of the prefects who jealously resented the development of a rival authority. Apart from the Paris region, the police remained essentially the potent auxiliaries of the prefects in their domination of the departments.

What place, finally, did Louis Napoleon allot to the army and the Church within his 'new system'?

In his message to the Legislative Body in June 1852 at the end of its first session he specifically referred to his government as resting 'on the people, the source of all power; on the army, source of all force; on religion, source of all justice'. The army had been the instrument with which he had executed the *coup d'état*; it cherished the memory of Napoleon and in 1852 acclaimed the Empire even before it was restored. No Bonapartist ruler could ignore it, and after December 2, 1851, Louis Napoleon at once showed his gratitude by a special proclamation and by restoring to it something of the pride of place and social prestige it had enjoyed before 1815. Its material and moral conditions were improved. He gave it the right to vote; the pay of non-commissioned officers was increased; he instituted a Military Medal, 'Souvenir of the Imperial Epic'—hitherto, in the words of General de Gaulle, 'never a decoration had adorned a trooper's breast'—and it carried with it a small annual pension; the Imperial Guard was eventually reconstituted, 'surrounding the Emperor as of old, wearing the same uniform and bearing the same flag'; and military reviews and ceremonies were a regular part of the display of a more colourful regime in which the ruler was to give his soldiers many opportunities to win new laurels on the battlefield.

The Austrian Ambassador, Hübner, writing within a month of the *coup d'état*, thought that, since its author's power was founded on the army, his motto should be 'Avec elle, par elle, pour elle'. But the *coup d'état* was no *pronunciamento* and the government of Napoleon III no military dictatorship. Once the army had completed its task of restoring order, the civilian powers resumed control and the army returned to the role to which it had become accustomed during the preceding thirty years, that of serving as 'a passive instrument in the hands of authority, a simple agent executing the decisions of the government'. Although the colonels of the Paris garrison after Orsini's attempt on the Emperor's life in 1858 might roundly declare that the army was called on to play a political role in times of crisis, it was not a Bonapartist instrument, whatever the sympathies of individual soldiers. The Second Empire depended on it in the last resort for the maintenance of order, just as had the governments of the Restoration and July Monarchies, but when the Legislative Body dethroned the Emperor in September 1870 and proclaimed a Republic, the troops still free to move accepted the political change and made no attempt to resist on behalf of their fallen chief.

The position of the Church was more complicated. The sceptical Napoleon I, who had regarded religion as an indispensable social cement, had quickly seen its political importance and the expediency of putting an end to religious strife by agreement with Rome. Napoleon III, who was also probably personally indifferent in religion, was no less aware of the great social and political power of the Church. Although religious practice had declined in many parts of France and anti-clericalism was latent or overt in certain milieux, the Church had strikingly demonstrated its influence in 1848. It was under the guidance of the curés and in accordance with the directives of the Catholic electoral committee organized by Montalembert that many of the peasantry had gone to the polls; and it was to the Church that many of the leading bourgeois politicians, such as Thiers and Cousin, abandoning the Voltairianism so characteristic of the middle classes in the first half of the century, had turned for support against the menaces of social disorder and socialism. As the Catholic voters had been an important element in Louis Napoleon's election victory in 1848, so the continued alliance of these two conspicuous champions of order was only natural after the *coup d'état* and the restoration of the Empire. As Prince-President, Louis Napoleon in his speeches had frequently emphasized the importance of the Church and shown his respect for religion; he had countenaneed the Loi Falloux and facilitated the return of the Pope to Rome. Now, as Emperor, it was also his policy during the first years of his reign to shower benefits upon the clergy. In consequence, their material wealth much increased, their schools and influence in education multiplied, and the numbers of religious orders were greatly augmented. As a result, he was assured of the support of a large majority of Catholics so long as his enterprises did not offend any of their fundamental tenets or loyalties; that there was a minority of unrepentent Legitimists or of Liberal Catholics like Montalembert, who soon became disillusioned by the authoritarian and seemingly Ultramontane sympathies of the new regime, did not greatly matter. The Gallican Church had seldom been without its internal differences and had seldom been free from intransigent groups who were opposed to the government policies of the day. Thus the alliance of Throne and Altar, an uncomfortable marriage of expediency rather than a close union of conviction as in the days of Charles X, was one of the conspicuous features of the years when the Empire was at its most authoritarian, and, even though Napoleon III broke loose from it towards the middle of his reign, Catholic opinion was too important a factor for him ever to be able to ignore it completely.

The result of the plebiscite following the *coup d'état* made the restoration of the Empire a foregone conclusion, but although Louis Napoleon moved at once from the Elysée to the royal palace of the Tuileries, assumed semi-royal state, allowed Imperial emblems to reappear and Republican ones to vanish, and authorized August 15th, the anniversary of

Napoleon's birthday, to be observed as a national festival, he proceeded again with his usual caution. Before committing himself, he preferred to sound opinion at home still further and to strengthen himself in view of possible hostility abroad by making an autumnal tour of the provinces and obtaining a fresh mandate from 'the people, the source of all power'. The tour, carefully organized by the prefects, was an increasingly triumphal progress, which culminated in a visit to Bordeaux, once a fortress of royalism. There the President felt strong enough to come out into the open. In a famous speech he declared that, because she desired confidence in the present and security for the future, France 'seemed to wish to return to the Empire' and that the Empire meant not war, but peace and economic development. After this there could be no doubt about the restoration. On November 7 a *Sénatus-Consulte* proposed the necessary constitutional modifications, and on the 20th another plebiscite recorded a vote of nearly eight millions in favour of the Empire. In raising to the throne a man who in so many ways represented 'the cause of the people and the national will', he told his Senators, the nation would 'crown itself'. On December 1, 1852, Louis Napoleon, the one time conspirator and prisoner at Ham, abandoning 'the modest title of President', became Emperor of the French as 'Napoleon III', and on the morrow, the anniversary both of the *coup d'état* and of Austerlitz, he made a formal entry into the capital of this restored Empire. The ambition cherished for twenty years was at last achieved.

But the nephew, who thus followed in his uncle's footsteps, failed to emulate him further by bringing the Pope to Paris for his coronation and by marrying into one of the old-established dynasties. Negotiations with the Pope broke down, despite what Pius IX called 'a magnificent letter' from Napoleon in July 1853, because Pius's price, the abolition of the Organic Articles instituted by Napoleon I, was too high for Napoleon III to pay. The Organic Articles were a powerful weapon in the hands of the State for the control of the Church and no previous French Government, not even that of the bigoted Charles X, had been willing to relinquish them. Napoleon III could certainly not have afforded to do so, for public opinion in France, where the old Gallican mistrust of Rome had been roused anew by Pius IX's support of French Ultramontanes, would have been bitterly opposed to such a surrender. The failure, however, may have rankled with him, for although relations between Church and State remained outwardly friendly for some time to come, after this check to his ambitions they were no longer suffused with their former warmth.

A little earlier, negotiations which had been discreetly entered upon with various courts during 1852 to provide the would-be Emperor with a royal bride had also come to nothing. But this setback did not long delay his marriage. Less than two months after he became Emperor, Napoleon III announced his forthcoming union with a lovely auburn-haired twenty-seven year old Spaniard, the Countess Eugénie de Montijo, with whom he had recently become infatuated. Conventional circles were horrified by what they regarded as this fresh proof of the Emperor's headstrong nature and readiness to defy public opinion. But Napoleon advisedly made the best of the situation in a speech to the Senate and other public bodies, in which he declared that, when one had been 'elevated by a new principle to the height of the ancient dynasties', one did not 'become acceptable merely by giving a greater antiquity to one's escutcheon and seeking to thrust one's way into the family of kings at any cost'. On the contrary, acceptability was achieved by 'always being mindful of one's origin, by preserving one's own character, and by truly adopting vis-à-vis Europe the position of a *parvenu*, a glorious title when it has been obtained through the free votes of a great people'.

The marriage took place on January 30, 1853, and three years later the Empress gave birth to their only child, the Prince Imperial. All being well, the succession was assured. With this 'Enfant de France', the Emperor told the Senators, there was born 'an heir destined to perpetuate a national system', not merely the child of a family but 'the son of the whole country'.

Meanwhile, a splendid and elaborate, though far from rigid, court had been established, centred on the Tuileries or the residences at St. Cloud and Compiègne, which Napoleon and

Eugénie liked most to frequent. But the panoply of the court and the beauty of the Empress did not compensate for her lack of royal blood, and throughout the reign the old French families tended to shun the Tuileries as they had shunned the Elysée. The 'parvenu's' court was attended mainly by new adherents of the regime, members of Napoleon I's new aristocracy and large numbers of foreigners.

The Empress who presided over it was a woman of great character and goodwill who carried out her public duties with admirable dignity and bore with fortitude the infidelities of her husband and the calamities which later were to crowd upon her. Vivacious and *mondaine*, yet profoundly devout, she none the less lacked the qualities which might best have compensated for her want of royal lineage. The ideal wife for a man like Napoleon III would have been a woman of cultivation with the width of intelligence and soundness of judgment to enable her to be a helping and steadying confidante for him in his political plans. Eugénie, however, was neither cultivated and intelligent nor sound in her political judgment; and though at first she exercised no political influence, later, when the Emperor was ageing and sick and the Prince Imperial growing up, she sought to do so with effects that were unfortunate.

Around the Emperor and Empress in the imperial family circle there were few persons of real importance. Napoleon III, once chided by his cousin who said that he had nothing of a Napoleon about him, replied, 'You are wrong. I have his family.' But more fortunate than his uncle, without his large, indocile and rapacious set of brothers, sisters, and relations, Napoleon III had only an aged uncle and cousins and illegitimate kinsmen to consider and no thrones to bestow. The uncle, Jerome, ex-King of Westphalia, he settled in the dignified sinecure of Governor of the Invalides. Among the cousins it was Jerome's two children who counted, Princess Mathilde, the family's chief patroness of literature and the arts, who kept aloof from politics but always remained on affectionate terms with Napoleon III, despite her resentment of his marriage, and her tempestuous brother Prince Napoleon. More Napoleonic in appearance than any of the other men in the family, Plon-Plon, as he was popularly known, was its *enfant terrible*, intelligent and imperious, fanatically anti-clerical, a former deputy of the Mountain who continued to parade his Jacobin sympathies, an incalculable and embarrassing figure, ready to serve his cousin on important missions, and as eager as he to remake the European map, often discomfiting him by ill-timed sallies, yet fitfully exercising an undoubted influence. For him Napoleon would negotiate a dynastic marriage and toy with the idea of creating a kingdom in Poland or Central Italy.

Very different were the two illegitimate kinsmen of any significance, Morny and Walewski. Both had had political experience under Louis Philippe, both were passionate speculators, greedy for money, but Morny, the amoral and cynical grandson of Talleyrand, was vastly superior in intelligence and more liberal in outlook than the Austrophil diplomat Walewski, the offspring of the great Emperor's liaison with a fair Polish Countess. Both, however, served the Emperor faithfully until they died, Morny above all as the distinguished President of the Legislative Body, Walewski mainly in foreign affairs.

Apart from the family circle, virtually all the individuals who were to play leading roles in the government of the Empire —for they were individuals and never formed a clearly defined group—were already on the scene. Except for Persigny, the earliest disciple, they had all been tried as ministers or prefects during the Second Republic. They were to change little, while, amongst the intimate friends of the sovereign, faces long familiar to him were predominant, Hortense Cornu, his childhood playmate, who was also his goddaughter, Dr. Conneau, who had been with him at Boulogne and Ham, Mocquard, his chief secretary, who had once been at his father's court, Arese, his early Italian friend, and a number of Corsicans patronized by Jerome and his family. Such were the people about the new Emperor, men who had risen because of their kinship with him, men who had served him when he was Pretender, adherents of the Bonaparte family, and political opportunists who had hitched their wagon to the rising star, a motley collection, most of whom were neither aristocrats nor, though some were to be ennobled, particularly intended by the Emperor to form a new aristocracy like that of Napoleon I. It remained to be seen what he and they would make of their new order and whether they could disprove Mazzini's assertion of 1849 that new dynasties in Europe were no longer possible.

Although the institutions of the new system were modelled on those of the Consulate, Louis Napoleon had no intention of being content with what he once called 'a mean imitation of some past epoch'. He wished like his uncle 'to close the era of revolutions' and put an end to the strife of parties, not merely in order to enjoy personal power but also in order to achieve constructive ends. He wished to further France's social and economic development, not only because he believed that material progress would compensate his people for their loss of political liberty, but also because of his undoubtedly genuine awareness that there was room for immense improvement and that France was lagging behind some of her neighbours, because she was inadequately equipped with the means to exploit her great resources. He hoped, too, to succeed where Napoleon I had failed by ending the cleavages which had rent French society since the great revolution and by rallying all sections of opinion in support of a regime that was solid and durable. This was indeed an aim which, if it could be achieved, would be of lasting value and give France a strength and confidence such as she had not known for decades.

That this involved another problem, no less great and no less difficult, Louis Napoleon was also aware: it was the problem of reconciling authority and liberty.

The system he intended to create, he had said on December 31, 1851, would reconstitute authority without impairing equality. This was not difficult—the principle of equality before the law was maintained, universal suffrage was re-established and, like Napoleon, he was prepared to employ men of talent, no matter what their political antecedents. But, as in *Des Idées Napoléoniennes* he had declared that, had Napoleon I been able to retain power, his government would more than any other have been able to bring liberty, so in this same speech of December 1851 he had spoken of his own regime as 'not closing the door in any way to improvement' and as laying the foundations 'of the only structure capable later of supporting a wise and beneficent liberty'. His government, accordingly, was to move in the opposite direction from those of the Restoration and July Monarchies. They had been comparatively liberal but, as time went on, became increasingly reactionary. His system, possessing a flexibility theirs had not known, was to attempt and partly to achieve the far more difficult evolution from authoritarianism to liberalism, peacefully without revolution from below. For the time being, however, the manner of this evolution was a problem for the future. Political life was stilled and the whole emphasis of the first and most successful years of the reign lay not on internal politics but on economic development and on foreign policy. Early in 1859 the Emperor could still defend his authoritarian system in the following remarkable words in a letter to Walewski: 'If I do not represent the French Revolution I represent nothing and Henri V [the Comte de Chambord] should be in my place. Mine is a representative government with a freely elected Chamber voting laws and taxes. I am a sovereign possessing a civil list and I do not dip into the public purse whenever I like. We possess the *Code Napoléon* assuring everybody's rights and equality before the law; an independent judiciary; the opening of all posts; an army composed of the élite of the nation and no longer of mercenaries; there is liberty to write, think and believe within the limits of the law. Thus, when the peoples of Europe make revolutions to obtain the blessings we possess— and which they only obtained for a brief space under the Empire as the fruit of our victories—they naturally look to me because I represent these ideas, which are not yet the common property of Europe and which have been impeded by an impious sect which confounds '89 with '93. I repeat all this because my Ministers should always fully understand these fundamental ideas. I should like you to re-read my *Idées Napoléoniennes* which I wrote in 1837. My convictions have not changed.'

Chapter Four

The Economic *Coup d'État*

LOUIS NAPOLEON'S assertion in *Des Idées Napoléoniennes* that the Napoleonic idea was a social, industrial, commercial and humanitarian idea was no piece of idle rhetoric. It reflected his own profound beliefs and aspirations and also, perhaps, the influence upon him of one of the most modern and influential schools of political thought in France. No nineteenth-century sovereign would so eagerly pursue a policy of industrial and commercial expansion and social betterment; no other could have earned the name that Sainte-Beuve bestowed upon him of 'Saint-Simon on horse-back'.

The great apostles of economic development in France were the Saint-Simonians, followers of the eccentric but far-seeing Comte Henri de Saint-Simon (1760–1825), whose works had affirmed the primacy of economic production over the 'out-worn comedy' of politics and party struggles, and whose ideas fertilized almost all social and economic thought in the second quarter of the nineteenth century. Historians have not been able to determine with precision the extent of the Saint-Simonians' influence upon Louis Napoleon before he came to power, but it is known that he had read books by some members of the school, notably Michel Chevalier, as well as by English liberal theorists such as Ricardo and Bentham. He had written on sugar beet, agricultural colonies and the problem of a trans-isthmian canal in Central America. He had, like his brother, long been interested in machines, he had toured the industrial areas of England, he had followed the free trade debates in the English Parliament, and in a variety of ways he had shown his keen awareness of the importance of industrial and commercial power. Thus, even though his knowledge of finance and political economy was perhaps rudimentary, he would as Emperor more than once declare that it was the duty of good citizens to disseminate everywhere the sane doctrines of political economy. Thus, too, it is not surprising that, always interested in new ideas and determined to 'march with them', he was ready to back the Saint-Simonian innovators, who regarded the progress of material interests as 'to the highest degree a political matter', and many of whom had by the time of the *coup d'état* already become figures of note in the business world. Under his patronage during the Second Empire these men, the Péreires, the Talabots, de Lesseps, Michel Chevalier and others, exercised a remarkable influence.

Indeed, alongside 'the people, the church and the army', it was the businessmen and financiers who were the mainstay of Napoleon's regime and who enabled it to work its most solid achievements. The bourgeoisie who backed Louis Napoleon because he was their saviour from Socialism would also support him to a considerable degree, particularly in the first years of his reign, because of his deep concern for economic development and because they believed that he was as protectionist as they. A French writer has noted the interesting point that as early as the elections for the Legislative Assembly in 1849 the Bonapartists had spoken a different language from the other groups on the Right. While the themes of the latter were order, the family, property, and religion, the Bonapartists' talk was largely of country roads, canals and railways. So, too, it was significant that the petitions for constitutional revision in 1851 had been organized by a committee, not of politicians, but of business men. In many of the speeches on his provincial tours as Prince-President Louis Napoleon himself had emphasised the urgency of improvements in communications and commerce and industry, and he had concluded his famous speech at Bordeaux, heralding the Empire, by outlining the peaceful conquests before it: 'We have immense uncultivated areas to reclaim, roads to open, harbours to dig, rivers to make navigable, canals to finish, our railway network to complete . . . We have to bring our great Western ports nearer to the American continent by accelerating the communications we still lack.' This was the announcement of a great programme of public

works which was to make the unemployment of the Second
Republic seem a bad dream and which was to be one of the
finest achievements of his reign.

By the time he had spoken these words economic revival
was already under way. Louis Napoleon benefited from a
coincidence of favourable economic and technical circumstances which offered opportunities for a development which
has been called 'unique in the history of several centuries'. New
means of transport in the form of railways and steamboats were
now at hand to provide an unparalleled acceleration of movement and to offer the prospect of far wider markets. Prices,
which from 1815 to 1850 had tended to fall, now rose, as the
result of the discovery of the new goldfields in California and
Australia, and this trend continued steadily but moderately
throughout Napoleon's reign. This sudden increase in the
world's gold supplies could fortunately be absorbed without
the violent dislocations which would have occurred in earlier
times because there was an unprecedented demand for capital
to finance new developments. Given stability, the '50s and '60s
might thus have been a period of considerable prosperity for
France, whatever her form of government. In fact, however, it
was Louis Napoleon who, by the *coup d'état*, ensured political
stability. He, too, had a share in promoting an economic
expansion that during the first five years of his reign was
unmatched by any other state; for he recognized the importance of credit, which he had once called 'the moral aspect of
material interests', and he supported the Saint-Simonians, who
evolved the new techniques for providing credit and for
mobilizing capital. The impetus given by the restoration of
confidence was all the greater because the *coup d'état* freed
speculative forces which had for long been restrained by the
timid policies of the July Monarchy and by the political
troubles and uncertainties of the Second Republic.

The year 1852 was an *annus mirabilis* in the history of the
French economy. The Bank of France lowered its interest rates,
thus enabling promoters to borrow more cheaply and embarked
on a policy whereby, as in England, the bank rate could be
used as a means of economic control. The private banking
system, hitherto in the hands of a small number of conservative

firms like the Rothschilds, whose dealings were mainly in government funds, was transformed by the foundation of the Crédit Foncier in February and of the Crédit Mobilier in November. The first provided loans for improvement in landed property and had in fact more effect upon urban development and the financing of public works in Paris and in other big towns than on agriculture. The second, which counted among its promoters such close associates of the Prince-President as Morny, Persigny, Fould, and the Péreire brothers, as well as a number of foreign bankers, provided the same facilities for industry and commerce. It met with an immediate and astonishing success; its shares soon quadrupled in value, and, before long, it had wide ramifications, financing new enterprises in many parts of Europe as well as in France.

As a result of these new developments, the Paris of Napoleon III became the financial centre of Europe and its Bourse a rival to the City of London. Moreover, the international connexions of the French Rothschilds enabled them, too, to play a considerable part in developing mines in Austria, and railways in Switzerland, North Italy and Western Spain, while it was the success of their rivals of the Crédit Mobilier which stimulated the Austrian branch of the family to establish their great Creditanstalt in Vienna. In all this it is noteworthy that Napoleon III's government, in contrast to the governments of the Third Republic, made little effort to interfere with the volume and direction of the flow of capital. In this, as in other directions, it was a conspicuous protagonist of economic freedom.

The favourable political and economic climate enabled these new banks and other later foundations such as the Société Générale de Crédit Industriel et Commercial (1859) and the Crédit Lyonnais deposit bank (1863), to tap the huge monetary reserves represented by the savings of small men. Under the Second Empire such men, instead of hoarding their money or entrusting it only to the government, found that investment in railways and other public works was both safe and remunerative, and their emergence as investors marked the rise of 'the new social strata' who were to be so important in the Third Republic. So there began by means of what a French historian,

M. Louis Girard, has called 'the universal suffrage of capital' 'a constant plebiscite in favour of the policy of public works'. The financial methods were unorthodox and broke with the accounting habits of parliamentary states, for the system was an industrial and commercial rather than a governmental one —Napoleon's government did not itself give money to the companies, for it could not afford to do so—and it mortgaged the future in order to be able to ensure rapid development in the present. A future made prosperous by the public works of the present might well, it was hoped, be able to support the charges that those works incurred.

Throughout his period of power after the *coup d'état* Napoleon was particularly eager to give an impetus to trade by extending France's system of communications. Here, too, he lost no time. 1852 saw also the grant of concessions for the completion of some of the main trunk railways and, with state encouragement, the beginning of the merger of some of the many small private companies, established under the July Monarchy, into the six large companies which by 1857 controlled the national railway system. A great new era of railway building was thus begun, which gave a fresh lease of life to France's metallurgical industries and rapidly enlarged the home market for consumer goods. Already by 1857 most of the main lines were finished, linking Paris with different parts of the country and with Belgium, Spain, Germany and Italy. 1852 witnessed also the foundation of the first big Parisian store, the *Bon Marché*, the digging of the first pit of the great new north-eastern coalfield at Lens and the coming of a new era for the Alsatian textile industry with the setting up at Mulhouse of the first modern loom with self-acting spindles. It was a year, too, in which measures were taken to hasten on a national telegraph system and in which Louis Napoleon showed his concern for urban development. Little interested in literature, music, or the visual arts, despite an early competence in drawing, he took a keen personal interest in town planning and in architecture. So in 1852 one of his first acts was to improve his capital by accelerating the completion of his uncle's notable Rue de Rivoli, by ordering the joining of the Palace of the Tuileries to the Louvre, and

Communications 1852–70

by furthering the construction of the Central Markets or Halles. These he insisted on having made in the newest building material, namely iron, of which one of the architects whom he particularly favoured, Viollet-le-Duc, the celebrated restorer of ancient monuments, was a passionate advocate.

In the same year, moreover, in the course of a visit to Marseilles, now to be the terminus of the great P.L.M. trunk railway, he approved the principles of a reconstruction which would, with what was regarded as 'American rapidity', transform that ancient city into 'the best and busiest port of France' and of the whole Mediterranean. Whether or not he had read Michel Chevalier's articles in the *Globe* on a 'Mediterranean System' twenty years earlier, he was indeed helping to promote the kind of development Chevalier had envisaged—a development of rapid communication between west and east by means of a network of railroads, connected with steamship lines and financed by a chain of banks. This plan for Marseilles, moreover, was not a purely economic measure, but part of a design to secure a hegemony in the Mediterranean sea and make it a French lake.

All this was the prelude to further creations and expansion. Along with the railways went the improvement of country roads and the development of overseas communications. The Messageries Maritimes, founded already in 1851 and constantly supported by Napoleon, became the chief rivals of the English P. and O., carrying French mails to Italy, the Levant and Algeria, and then still further afield to the Black Sea, South America and the Far East. Soon they were to build their own ships and become by far the largest carriers in the Mediterranean. In 1855 there followed the establishment by the Péreire brothers of the Compagnie Générale Maritime, which promoted a notable development of the port of Le Havre and in 1864 added to its imports of fertilizers and nitrates from South America a regular passenger service to New York. Trade with South America and the Far East, hitherto spasmodic, now became increasingly important. These and other developments were such that the combined value of France's imports and exports was nearly trebled before the Empire fell. This, too, was a rate of increase unsurpassed elsewhere and an achievement of which the Emperor was justly proud. Along with the growing demand for machinery went a great advance in the use of metals, the introduction of new techniques, especially coke smelting in the metallurgical industries, and increases in the production and consumption of coal, coke, and steel, all of which approximately doubled in the decade 1850–60.

While the greater part of this expansion was the work of private companies, Napoleon and his ministers did their part in encouraging it. Agricultural institutes and model farms were founded and courses were instituted to teach new agricultural and industrial techniques, with the very important consequence that France no longer needed to import English technicians and skilled labour. She could produce her own. Legislation was passed to facilitate land reclamation and drainage, in which the Emperor himself took special interest. The great shipping companies were subsidised and five transatlantic lines were organized by a law of 1857, the railway companies were required to develop branch lines, the canals in private hands were purchased in order to maintain a national system of waterways which would not be put out of business by the railways, and laws of 1865 and 1867 enabled the establishment of limited liability companies and of 'sociétés anonymes'.

To the general public in France and the outside world this economic dynamism of the new Empire was made known above all by the Paris Exhibition of 1855. Here, as so often in economic and social matters, Napoleon took a leaf out of England's book. England, once again the pioneer, had held the first international exhibition at the Crystal Palace in 1851. This had been proclaimed by the Prince Consort as one of those events 'in a period of most wonderful transition' which tended towards 'the realization of the unity of mankind'. Such a conception could not but appeal to Napoleon and he was determined that France, too, should make a similar gesture which would redound to the prestige both of the regime and of France's economy. He did not allow the Crimean War to interfere with his programme, and in 1855 he personally opened the exhibition with the full splendour of imperial pomp. Thus, as he did not fail to emphasize, it was a pacific gesture in the midst of war, and accordingly it was hailed as 'a

temple of peace' as well as an 'Olympiad of industry'. It
attracted no fewer than five million visitors, including Queen
Victoria and many other sovereigns. It did much to stimulate
French interest in new inventions. Nearly half the 24,000
exhibitors were French and many of the French exhibits, including locomotives, powerfully demonstrated that the France of
Napoleon III was a far more vigorous and progressive country
than the France of Louis Philippe or the Second Republic.

Yet it would be wrong to suppose that the first years of the
Second Empire were a time of universal well-being. There were
serious outbreaks of cholera in 1853–5 and the agricultural
picture was far from happy, for vines and potatoes were
ravaged by disease, the valleys of the Garonne and the Rhône
were flooded, and there was a run of bad harvests from 1853
to 1855 which led to a serious food crisis. Moreover, the collapse in 1857 of the general boom following the gold discoveries
hit France as well as many other countries and caused much
hardship. This Napoleon did his best to mitigate, for instance
by allocating contracts for his new naval programme in such a
way as to stimulate the metallurgical industries and by dis-
tributing those for armour plate as widely as possible. But the
really prosperous years were the middle years of the Empire
from 1858 to 1862.

The man who presided over this great expansion, the
Emperor, took a close personal interest in many of its aspects,
in the founding of the Crédit Foncier, for instance, and the
programme of railway construction; but nowhere was his personal responsibility more marked and more decisive than in the
transformation of Paris and in the liberalization of trade.

Napoleon I had begun to give his capital an imperial splendour, but many of his projects were unfinished or not begun
when he fell. Despite the new building which took place
between 1820 and 1846 and various plans for improvement,
Paris in 1851 was still in large part a sordid labyrinth of
narrow ill-lit streets and insanitary dwellings, huddled close
together and quite unfitted to serve a population that in nine
years was to increase by seventy per cent. Napoleon III now
set out to fulfil a long-cherished ambition, namely to complete
his uncle's work and to improve on it by making the city, now

the pivot of the country's railway system, not only still more splendid and far more spacious, but a great commercial centre, modern and hygienic, able to cope with the vast new influxes of settlers, goods, and visitors. Such a plan would redound to the prestige of the regime; it would also stimulate the economy and reduce the dangers of insurrection by making it much less easy to erect barriers across the new wide streets. The undertaking was, however, tremendous.

Fortunately, in appointing Haussmann to the post of Prefect of Paris in 1853, the Emperor found the perfect instrument for a task which, if it was to succeed in any foreseeable time, needed a man of immense drive and determination, able to surmount the opposition of countless vested interests. The two men worked in harmony for seventeen years. They spent long hours together in a small room in the Tuileries with tables covered with drawings and maps, Napoleon himself often personally suggesting the plans of new streets and boulevards and insisting that Paris, like London, should have its parks and garden squares. Thus, strong in the Emperor's support, Haussmann supervised or initiated the works which made Paris in large part the city we still know to-day with its broad avenues, great buildings such as the Halles and the Opéra, public gardens and squares, markets, aqueducts, sewers and railway stations. The new boulevards were the most famous contribution of the age to town-planning and the new lay-out of Paris was to influence such planning in many other cities from Rome and Madrid to Mexico City. Contemporaries were full of enthusiasm. Palmerston, on a visit in 1858, wrote that the Emperor was 'following the career of Augustus' and would 'do much more for the prosperity of France than the Roman Emperor did for the Roman Empire.' The cost was indeed enormous—the debts incurred were not finally discharged until 1929—yet even some of Haussmann's fiercest critics in the end paid tribute to his work. For instance, the Republican Jules Simon could say in 1882: 'It is of little importance to us to-day that the accounts of Haussmann were fantastic. He had undertaken to make Paris a magnificent city and he completely succeeded'; and an administrator and historian of Paris, M. Morizet, could write in 1932: 'All that was done needed to be done and certainly would not be done now if it had not been done sixty years ago.'

This transformation, however, entailed consequences not all of which were beneficial. In order to reduce the number of discontented people in the city, Napoleon had at one time contemplated prohibiting the building of more factories there. This had not been feasible; instead the rebuilding in the centre of Paris tended to thrust the workers into the peripheral quarters of the city so that the dichotomy between the middle-class and poorer quarters became more marked. The enlargement of the city meant to some extent the loss of social unity and the social problem presented by the suburbs was accentuated. Moreover, while Paris, with its museums, new theatres, exhibitions, and great stores like the Louvre, the Bon Marché, and the Samaritaine, became more than ever a cosmopolitan city, a Babylon or Babel in the eyes of some contemporaries, attracting visitors bent on pleasure from all over the world, it is arguable that its increasing dominance in all spheres of activity produced a disequilibrium which Napoleon did not foresee and which was unhealthy for the country as a whole. As M. Gaxotte has put it: 'just when industrialization was gaining momentum in its modern form it ensured to Paris . . . a privileged position which made of it almost the only financial and banking centre, a centre of commerce that was unnaturally inflated and a paradoxical centre of heavy industry', paradoxical because it was neither a seaport nor near the centres of coal and steel. The lure of Paris contributed to the depopulation of certain rural areas and increased 'the general costs of transportation, administration and police'.

France, traditionally protectionist since the days of Colbert, had become even more so since 1815. Industrialists and agriculturists alike regarded protection as part of the established order which Louis Napoleon, whose early essay on sugar-beet had been strongly protectionist, had come to save in 1851. But here, as in a number of other issues, the bourgeoisie misunderstood their ruler who (at least once in a speech at Lyon in 1850), while referring to the protection of industry, had spoken also of his wish to 'develop the exchange of products by a pro-

gressively liberal commercial system', and who was reported in
1852 to incline towards protection, but to be 'so anxious to
promote the welfare of the people' that he would go far to
promote free trade if urged to by his ministers. Louis Napoleon,
in fact, had once again been impressed by the example of
England. He wished, like Peel, to lower the cost of living for
the ordinary citizen and also to facilitate the import of
materials and equipment necessary to complete the programme
of railway building and industrialization. Moreover, he was
reminded by Chevalier, in a book trenchantly attacking the
protectionist system, that his uncle at St. Helena had declared
that men should 'fall back upon the free navigation of the
seas and the complete freedom of trade throughout the world'.
The fact that one of the constitutional modifications on which
he personally insisted when the Empire was proclaimed gave
the Emperor the power to conclude treaties of commerce without reference to the Legislative Body suggests that from the
outset he envisaged a possible move towards free trade as a
crowning of his economic structure, just as the possible concession of 'a wise and beneficent liberty' might one day crown
the political edifice.

Napoleon proceeded, however, with his usual caution, knowing the great strength of the protectionist interests. He con-
tented himself at first with decrees lowering the duties on the
import of materials essential to the programme of public works
and increased production such as coal and bar-iron (which
included rails (1853)), machinery (1855) and raw wool (1856).
In the middle 'fifties a recession, partly caused by the difficulties of the Crimean War, led him to seek to galvanize the
economy by a wider measure of liberalization. But the attempt
in 1856 to put through a proposal to lower tariffs met with so
much opposition from the protectionist interests in the Legislative Body that the bill was withdrawn. Napoleon, however,
warned the industrialists that the withdrawal was only in order
to gain them ample time in which to prepare themselves for a
more liberal regime.

Three years later the Emperor decided to make use of his
constitutional powers to conclude a commercial treaty with
England for the mutual lowering of tariffs. The initiative came

not indeed from him, but from Michel Chevalier, who saw in the dependence of Palmerston's new government on the political support of the Manchester free-traders an opportunity at last to make an agreement, and who enlisted the support of his friend Cobden and through him of Gladstone. On October 27, 1859, in separate interviews, Cobden and Chevalier persuaded the Emperor to approve their proposal which, after some understandable hesitations, he whole-heartedly backed. The negotiations were conducted with the greatest secrecy, largely by Michel Chevalier and Rouher on the one hand and by Cobden and Russell on the other, and the brusque announcement in January 1860 of their conclusion had something of the effect of an economic *coup d'état*. This was, moreover, not merely an isolated agreement. It was the first step in a deliberate policy which led Napoleon within the next few years to the conclusion of similar treaties with almost every European country except Russia. Thus it was a significant contribution towards the expansion of international trade. But in France itself many of the bourgeoisie who had so warmly welcomed Louis Napoleon's political coup of 1851 viewed the Emperor's economic coup of 1860 in a very different light. More eager by now for a restoration of political liberty, they had been deaf to the government's warning in 1856 and were infuriated by an economic liberty which exposed them to the cold winds of English competition. In consequence, the treaty, which was part of a wider scheme for giving fresh stimulus to the French economy, had the effect of increasing the difficulties which Napoleon, in what have been called the 'années tour-nantes' of the Empire, was beginning to meet on every hand.

peasant and by faith, and without the difficulty to reconcile
then extents of deacdotion, the Emperor faced in numerous
official points and in the thronging rumours of the Court
could not be fixed close mounting our regime to deserve a ...
minister and the late notices and monetary the dome of
bourned the hope is not certain and be a stream

Chapter Five

Foreign Policy: The Fortunate Years

FEW self-made rulers have resisted the temptation to pursue an ambitious foreign policy in the hope of achieving abroad the success which might aid consolidation at home. That such a course would be followed by Louis Napoleon was widely expected and widely feared, especially after the restoration of the Empire. His name, his adoption of the Napoleonic legend with its theme of a new European federation resting upon nationalities, his desire that his regime should have the lustre which the July Monarchy had so signally lacked, all suggested that such might be his aim and that he would seek to undermine the existing order based upon the treaties of 1815, which, he told the British Ambassador, were galling to France. But how this 'strange unaccountable man', who seemed to the Prince Consort to resemble 'a German savant rather than a sovereign of France', would go about his task and what were his ultimate intentions was indeed uncertain.

The uncertainty was all the greater because of the Emperor's remarkable self-control, his secretive character and his devious methods, and the belief of some that he never told the truth. What was to be made of this man whom the Austrian Ambassador described as able 'to express himself very well and sometimes with a real or simulated abandon', but who never entered into the arguments presented to him, whose immobility of feature formed 'an impenetrable mask and breastplate', and who left his interlocutor 'with the feeling of not having been understood', either because he did not want to understand or because he did not want it to be seen that he had understood? Moreover, the mask was often as impenetrable to his own ministers as to foreign envoys. Only very occasionally did he give way to an outburst of passion. Still a conspirator by temperament and by habit, and without the diligence to read more than extracts of despatches, the Emperor liked to employ unofficial agents and bypass the regular channels of the Foreign Ministry; he liked also to preserve the maximum flexibility of movement until the last moment, running with the hare and hunting with the hounds at the same time; he preferred methods that were clandestine, secret conciliabula and interviews at which he was the sole French negotiator. Thus, in the realm of foreign policy still more than in any other department of state, his ministers were often, as a French historian has said, 'not counsellors, but mere executors of designs of which they only see fragments'. A small but highly revealing example of the way in which he treated them is given in the diary of one of them. During the Crimean War, when it was known at the Council of Ministers that the Emperor was shortly to make an important pronouncement, the Minister of Justice made bold to ask if the speech would be warlike: 'The Emperor, a little surprised, replied: "Fairly". We thought he would have read it to us. He had already sent it to be printed'. Foreign policy thus was his peculiar prerogative, the Emperor's secret, just as it had been sometimes in the eighteenth century the 'secret of the King'.

In the past many historians sought to unlock the door to this secret with a single key. For Emile Bourgeois that key was the drive to 'do something' for Italy, for Hermann Oncken it was the ambition to recover the Rhine frontier, for Albert Pingaud the search for a grand alliance, for Heinrich von Sybel Mediterranean hegemony. But modern historians prefer the view that Napoleon III was too complex a character to have a single aim, and believe rather that he had several aims, by no means all compatible, and that he sought to achieve now one and now another according as opportunity offered. In any event, however, the achievement of some of these aims must entail upsetting the 1815 treaties. Men who wished to preserve the *status quo* were right in fearing that, for all his professions of peace, Napoleon's advent to power would entail a restless policy and precipitate an era of great changes in the European states system. Although others besides Cavour believed that while he never forgot a service, he never forgave an injury, it was not just the personal resentment of a 'parvenu' Emperor, who had failed to make a royal marriage and whom the conservative Powers were slow to recognize, that impelled him to policies that would change the European map.

At first, however, the obstacles to change seemed formidable. The great opportunity for France, had she been strong enough, to lead a movement of nationalities and peoples and to initiate a new European order had come early in 1848. But she had then wisely recognized that she was too weak. By the end of 1848, when Louis Napoleon was elected President, reaction was in full swing, and by the end of 1849 the old order had, with some constitutional and social modifications in certain parts of Europe, been re-established. The great powers, liberal England as much as the conservative 'Northern' courts of Austria, Russia, and Prussia, were as determined as ever to uphold the treaties of 1815, and France, an unstable Republic, with an uncertain future, was relatively isolated and suspect. Thus Louis Napoleon had at first little room for manoeuvre. But he had two great assets. Unlike his dynamic and impetuous uncle, he was possessed of infinite patience, and in France he more than anyone else came to represent order and stability. His patience meant that he was willing to wait and watch and probe, mindful perhaps of his mother's reputed advice to her sons long ago: 'Always watch the horizon . . . There is no . . . drama which . . . may not provide you with some motive for intervention, like a god in the theatre. Be everywhere, always patient, always free, and only show yourselves at the right time'. His being a 'man of order' meant that he earned the goodwill of conservative governments, who feared that prolonged unrest in France would lead to some new and more dangerously radical French revolution, and of business interests who saw in him the best hope of reviving trade. As the *Economist* wrote in November 1851, Louis Napoleon 'the guardian of Order' was 'recognised as such in every stock exchange in Europe'.

His patience did not, however, in any sense mean that he was content before becoming absolute master of France with a purely passive foreign policy. On the contrary. He quickly made it clear to his ministers that he expected to have a controlling say in the conduct of policy; he lost little time in testing some of the schemes which were stored up in the mind that Palmerston later described as 'like a rabbit warren'; and his government took its part in nearly every major issue that arose before his *coup d'état*. Thus in January 1849 he proposed to England a limitation of naval armaments and in March a general European congress to consider questions which threatened European peace; in June he despatched reinforcements to Rome and in August laid down his conditions for the Pope's return; in October he sent the French fleet to the Dardanelles to back England in her support of the Turks' resistance to the Austrian and Russian demands for the extradition of Polish and Hungarian refugees involved in the Hungarian revolt of 1849; in November he suggested to the Tsar a remodelling of Europe which involved the partitioning of Turkey and compensation for France on the Rhine; and in the following year he sounded both Prussia and Austria concerning schemes in which the price of French support would be perhaps the Bavarian Palatinate. In the early spring of 1850, when Palmerston high-handedly repudiated an agreement reached for the settlement of the claims against Greece of a Portuguese Jew named Don Pacifico, who claimed British citizenship, Louis Napoleon withdrew his ambassador from London. In July of the same year his government signed with Russia and Great Britain a protocol which recognized the Danish rule of inheritance in the duchies of Schleswig and Holstein. In the winter of 1850–1 he firmly opposed the inclusion of the whole Austrian empire within the Germanic Confederation on the ground that this would be a modification of the treaty of 1815.

Seen in perspective these varied examples of his early diplomatic activity are most revealing. They indicate his desire for peaceful change, his wish to stand well with England, his hostility to Austria, his concern for France's prestige, and his restless search for any possibility of territorial gain; all recurring themes in the next two decades.

It is significant that the first two important proposals put forward by Louis Napoleon were for peaceful change and that they were made to England. The first was, as F. A. Simpson has said, 'the most drastic proposal for the limitation of naval armaments ever put forward by the head of any nation'. France would be prepared to make almost any reduction that England suggested provided that England would also do so 'upon somewhat the relative scale'. So long as England and France understood one another, the French Foreign Minister explained, 'their respective fleets would be quite sufficient to ensure the respect of the rest of the world'. This was an idea to which Louis Napoleon was to revert in 1854 and, much later, in 1870, he made a similar proposal concerning land armaments to Prussia, then France's only serious military rival, as England was now her only serious rival at sea. The naval proposal, unprecedented in character, was politely turned down by Palmerston, who replied that England with her world-wide possessions could not make the size of her navy dependent on that of any other power. Nevertheless, as an earnest of his seriousness Louis Napoleon, despite strong opposition, succeeded in effecting considerable reductions of men and material in France's naval and military budget for 1849.

The other proposal met with equally short shrift from Palmerston. Louis Napoleon put it forward, characteristically without having consulted his ministers, in a confidential interview with Normanby, the British Ambassador. It was that the two governments should issue a joint invitation to the Powers to attend a general congress to consider all problems which threatened the peace of Europe. Evidently any such congress might entail modification of the treaties of 1815, but Louis Napoleon pointed out that these had already been violated on many occasions and that, if such a congress were now held to make changes in the European order, any new settlement which emerged would have the great advantage of France's wholehearted support. But in this proposal Palmerston saw the cloven hoof of French ambition, and he turned it down on the grounds that the only troubles at the moment were of an internal rather than an international character and that the principles of the two countries forbade them to interfere in internal problems.

However understandable the attitude of the British Government, it was unimaginative. Acceptance of the first proposal might well have averted the naval arms race that developed between the two countries at the end of the following decade, while a congress, though this is far more debatable, might have secured some recognition or guarantee of the rights of nationalities subject to foreign dominion. On the other hand, so far as Louis Napoleon was concerned, the proposals undoubtedly reflected his preference for what a great Englishman later called 'jaw-jaw rather than war-war'. But he would not shrink from war if congresses were unobtainable or unavailing and if he believed that national prestige or his own position at home demanded it.

It was significant that these proposals had been made to England. Whether or not this 'Saint-Simon on horseback' had read and been influenced by a book by Saint-Simon and Thierry, published in 1815, which had advocated alliance between England and France as the foundation for the reorganization of Europe, he had undoubtedly taken to heart the lessons of his uncle's career and recognized that it was England's unrelenting enmity that had been Napoleon I's undoing. He was determined not to make a similar mistake. Lord Malmesbury, the British Foreign Secretary, recognized this in October 1852 when he wrote: 'I believe that he is convinced that war with England lost his uncle his throne and that he *means* to try peace with us'. Louis Napoleon knew England's power, he admired her institutions and he had a genuine affection for the country in which he had spent so many years of exile and been so hospitably received. Thus it became clear very early that friendship with England would be a cardinal principle of his policy—the British Ambassador in November 1849, after the Anglo-French co-operation over the question of the Hungarian and Polish refugees, could even speak of 'the alliance with England' to which Louis Napoleon 'is above all other men in France most devotedly attached.' Such devotion, however, as the Don Pacifico affair showed, would not mean subservience.

Scarcely less marked was Louis Napoleon's dislike of Austria, the power who had been the chief architect of the 1815 treaties, who still dominated Northern Italy and who by her very nature must be the principal opponent of any attempt to re-fashion the European system on the basis of nationality. Austria, as he said much later, was 'a cabinet for whom I have always felt . . . the most lively repugnance', and in 1858 in negotiations with

Russia he would even propose her dismemberment. His government moved troops to Rome to forestall Austria in 1849; his action later that year in supporting Turkey in the question of the Hungarian refugees was a demonstration of hostility to Austria no less than of friendship for England; one may suppose, too, that he took a peculiar pleasure in protesting to Schwarzenberg against the proposed inclusion of the whole Austrian Empire in the Germanic Confederation on the ground that this would upset the European equilibrium 'consecrated by the general treaties'!

Louis Napoleon's *coup d'état*, viewed with alarm in liberal Belgium which sheltered many French refugees, had Orleanist connexions and feared invasion, was, however, widely welcomed elsewhere for the reasons already indicated, namely that it was good for trade and bad for radicalism. But the restoration of the Empire was a very different matter. The very name of Empire in France seemed to imply a threat to the 1815 settlement and its restoration meant the return of a dynasty which the Powers had refused to recognize. Thus, when the restoration seemed imminent in the spring of 1852, Russia and Prussia welcomed an Austrian proposal that the Powers should exact from the Emperor-to-be a guarantee of his peaceful intentions before they consented to accord him recognition. But Louis Napoleon partially disarmed them in October by his famous speech at Bordeaux declaring that the Empire meant peace; and he told the British Ambassador that, while he had every intention of observing the 1815 treaties, 'a public and solemn declaration that I recognize them might humiliate the French nation'. The British Government were content with this assurance, seeing that it would be useless to try to exact a formal declaration. But the solidarity of the Powers was maintained by their signature, on the morrow of the restoration, of a protocol in which they noted the new Emperor's peaceful professions and reaffirmed their intentions to uphold the territorial *status quo*. Although Napoleon III had thus avoided any public commitment to stand by the 1815 treaties, his assumption of the Imperial title appeared to have reunited the Allies of 1815 and to have emphasized anew France's isolation.

But this unity was fragile and a series of events soon occurred which enabled Napoleon to drive a wedge between the so-called 'Northern' courts, emerge from isolation and secure the much coveted alliance with England.

The first rift occurred over Napoleon's 'dynastic numeral'. The Tsar had been alarmed and antagonized more than any other sovereign by the restoration of the Empire and had personally tried to dissuade Louis Napoleon from taking such a step. Now his assumption of the style 'Napoleon III' seemed to Nicholas I an additional piece of arrogance, since the Allies had never recognized Napoleon II. Encouraged by Austria, the Tsar refused to treat Napoleon III as a legitimate sovereign, delayed in authorizing his ambassador to present his credentials, and then greeted the new ruler not in the traditional form as his 'brother' but merely as his 'friend'. At one moment it looked as though 'the dynastic numeral' would lead to a rupture of diplomatic relations, but Napoleon had the good sense not to let a matter of protocol provoke a crisis of such magnitude. He adroitly let the incident pass with a famous repartee: 'We have to put up with our brothers, but we can choose our friends'. The incident, moreover, turned to his advantage, for, when it came to the point, the rulers of Austria and Prussia had followed Queen Victoria and not the Tsar in giving Napoleon III recognition in the customary way. The significance of the rift was hardly likely to be lost on the new Emperor.

By the time that this flurry over the 'dynastic numeral' was at its height Franco-Russian relations had already deteriorated as a result of a religious dispute in the Near East. By the capitulations of 1740 Turkey had granted to France the right to protect the interests of Latin Christians in the Ottoman Empire. During the revolutionary and Napoleonic wars, however, preoccupied by greater matters, French Governments had done little to maintain the Latins' privileges, while the Orthodox, protected by Russia, had obtained concessions from the Porte which conflicted with those accorded to the Latins. In 1819 and subsequently under the July Monarchy France had made efforts, but only fitfully, to sustain the Latin positions. By the middle of the century, however, these assumed a greater importance in the eyes of a French Church reinvigorated and imbued with a new missionary spirit, and Louis Napoleon,

ready both to win favour with the Church and prestige
wherever it might be picked up, was not averse to championing them more boldly. By February 1852 he appeared to have
gained all that could be desired when the Turks conceded most
of his demands concerning Latin rights in the Holy Places in
Palestine. But under Russian pressure the Turks characteristically played a double game, simultaneously giving the Greeks
a *Firman* or edict approving and confirming their rights. The
dispute instead of being over had entered a new and more
acute phase in which French naval power, wider Russian
claims, Turkish nationalism, and English concern for the maintenance of the balance of power and the preservation of the
Ottoman Empire were the most important factors.

It was indeed galling to the Tsar that his prestige in the
Near East should be impaired by the actions of an upstart
Bonaparte and by Turkish prevarication. Early in 1853, after
toying with the idea of a sudden attack on Constantinople and
of a gentleman's agreement whereby England and Russia
should settle the affairs of the Near East together, he sent a
new special mission to Constantinople to demand satisfaction
in the Holy Places dispute and an agreement whereby Turkey
would confirm his right to act as Protector of her twelve million
Greek Orthodox subjects. Thanks to French conciliatoriness
and English good offices agreement was quickly reached over
the Holy Places. But that issue, on which, had he wished,
Napoleon III could probably have effected a retreat without
any further condemnation at home, was now completely
transcended by the Russian demand for a religious protectorate
which would have enabled her to intervene at any time in
Turkish affairs, thus making a mockery of Turkish independence. Both England and France regarded the demands as
inadmissible, although they did their best to keep the door
open for negotiations. Their efforts, however, broke down because of Turkish nationalist intransigence, which had already
been encouraged by the naval measures taken by France.

In the preceding year, 1852, when the Turks had begun to
shuffle over the implementation of their agreement with the
French concerning Latin rights, Louis Napoleon had sent first
a French fleet to Salamis and then the *Charlemagne*, a new

screw battleship, through the Dardanelles. In March 1853 when Menshikov, the Russian special envoy at Constantinople, had enforced the resignation of the Turkish Foreign Minister, Fuad Bey, and there was news of Russian military and naval preparations, the French Emperor had, acting independently of England, ordered French ships to Salamis. The French navy, which was to be such a notable force in the coming decade, had already impressed the Turks with the belief that France was a possible ally, who, either alone or with the added support of England, could help them to defeat the Russians. Sure now of English sympathy as well, they flatly rejected the Russian demands, although Menshikov had made some concessions. Negotiations were broken off at the end of May 1853 when Menshikov departed menacingly from Constantinople. Another in the long series of Russo-Turkish wars seemed imminent. Yet hostilities did not break out between these two ancient antagonists until October 1853 and, although the two powers ordered their fleets to Besika Bay as early as June 1853, fearing an immediate Russian attack on Constantinople, it was not until the end of March 1854 that France and England entered the war against Russia as allies of Turkey.

The length of time which elapsed before the outbreak of war is striking evidence of the desire of the Western Powers to avoid hostilities. There is no justification for the view, once malevolently put forward by Kinglake, one of his unsuccessful rivals for the affections of Miss Howard, that Napoleon III was the villain of the piece, the man who in machiavellian fashion engineered the Crimean War in order to maintain himself at home and to secure a position from which he could destroy the settlement of 1815. During the five months following the departure of the Menshikov mission from Constantinople Napoleon's representatives took an active part in negotiations at Vienna to work out an agreement acceptable to both Russia and Turkey. The resulting proposals, however, which were agreed to by Russia, fell through because of Turkish stubbornness and Russian clumsiness. When, in consequence, the Turks opened hostilities with an effort to drive the Russians out of the Principalities, which they had begun to occupy in June, Napoleon III expressed the hope that defeat would bring them to reason. Unfortunately the defeat they suffered was at sea and not on land. When a squadron of the Russian Black Sea Fleet annihilated a Turkish flotilla at Sinope soon after the British and French fleets had moved from Besika Bay to the Bosphorus their victory seemed a provocation to the maritime powers, especially England, where public opinion, much more strongly anti-Russian than in France, worked itself into a war-fever. In France, on the other hand, although Napoleon III at once reacted with strong measures in support of Turkey, Sinope had the effect for the first time of seriously arousing opinion to the dangers of a general war, for which it was soon evident that French businessmen and peasants had no enthusiasm. It was perhaps awareness of their opposition that led Napoleon III to make a last bid for peace and to write on January 29, 1854, a personal letter to the Tsar, which could have offered the Russian government the opportunity for a dignified retreat. But by then the French and British action in sending their fleets into the Black Sea to deny it to Russian but not to Turkish naval operations had injured Russian pride too deeply for accommodation. Although Austria and Prussia had so far refused his appeals for their support and the solidarity of the conservative powers looked like being a myth, the Tsar answered haughtily that Russia would be found the same in 1854 as in 1812.

In fact, Napoleon III's conduct had also been actuated largely by his desire to co-operate with England without merely following in her wake. Anglo-French relations had in some ways deteriorated since 1849 as a result of friction over Don Pacifico, French refugees, a supposed French threat to Belgium, and other matters. Now in bolstering up Turkey it was clear that England needed French support, and so Napoleon had an unrivalled opportunity to renew the Near Eastern 'alliance' of October 1849. But, as French opinion was highly susceptible so far as the old enemy was concerned, it was necessary for him not always to leave the initiative to England. Thus, while he had in the autumn of 1853 rejected a transparent attempt by Nicholas to detach him from England, he had taken the lead in urging the despatch of the joint fleets from Besika Bay to the Bosphorus and in subsequently insisting that they should enter the Black Sea to protect the Turkish ships and to immobilize the Russian Black Sea forces at Sebastopol. To a considerable extent the two Powers edged their way into war because, as has been said, 'they were drawn along from first to last by the need to prove to each other their mutual good faith'. It was Napoleon who took the last and fatal initiative concerning the Black Sea and it was France who declared war a day before England.

Once France and England were engaged side by side, a formal alliance was a natural consequence and this was concluded on April 10, 1854. The war was the first 'general' war since 1815 and Napoleon had effected a dramatic 'revolution in alliances'. But both sides sought to make it still more general by winning over Austria and Prussia, who wished to remain neutral. In December the Western Powers secured the alliance of Austria, though not her participation in the war, and Napoleon III was warmly congratulated by one of his ambassadors on having inflicted a mortal blow on the Holy Alliance, while in January they gained the more practical aid of Sardinia. To obtain the aid of both Austrians and Italians in the same cause seemed indeed a triumph for Western and particularly French diplomacy.

But these successes in negotiation were not matched in war. Early in 1853 Napoleon had hoped to confine the operations of the maritime powers to naval warfare and had said he would not send a single soldier to the East. But English representations soon persuaded him that armies must be raised as well as ships. Even before the declaration of war he had suggested that hostilities should open with a combined attack by land and sea on Sebastopol, but the proposal had been turned down by the English experts and it was not until five months later, after the failure of operations in the Baltic, that, foiled of a battlefield in the Principalities, the Allies turned in earnest to the Crimea. Unfortunately, the surprise attack which they launched against Sebastopol failed owing to poor generalship, and their armies, ravaged by disease and inadequately equipped and serviced for a lengthy campaign, had to settle down to the miseries of a prolonged siege. More and more reinforcements had to be sent and the prolongation of hostilities, combined with the bad

harvests of 1854 and 1855 and an economic recession, meant
that the war became increasingly unpopular in France. As early
as March 1855 the British Ambassador reported that though
the Emperor was still 'very firm', with everyone else the desire
was for '*paix à tout prix*'. Napoleon, in fact, was as good as
his word not to recede until a 'great success' had been obtained.
He was ready to go to the Crimea himself in order to galvanize
the troops. He was active in strengthening the alliance with
England, inviting the Prince Consort to Boulogne in September
1854, visiting Windsor and 'quite fascinating' Queen Victoria
in April 1855, and receiving a return visit in the autumn of the
same year—a stay which the Queen 'enjoyed beyond measure'.
Moreover, there is much to be said for the view that he was
the only man on the Allied side who appreciated the technical
and strategic needs of modern war. He was tireless in urging
the co-ordination of the Allied military effort and, although he
vainly pressed for a joint command for all operations, a remarkable co-operation was achieved in the building of ships
and exchange of naval plans. Furthermore, he himself contributed notably to the final series of successes when light
armoured floating batteries of his devising were successfully put
to the test at Kinburn in October 1855.

By then the tables had turned. Nicholas I had died in March
and his successor Alexander II was a less intransigent personality. In September the Russians, who were beginning to
feel the strain of prolonged war, abandoned Sebastopol. Although Napoleon III discussed further plans for new campaigns against Cronstadt and in the Caucasus, there is little
doubt that the economic and financial position in France, together with pressure from Russophils like Morny and reports
of the state of French public opinion, had, by the autumn of
1855, led him to wish to end the war as quickly as possible. He
cared less for the fate of Turkey (which he did not even mention in his message to the Legislative Body in March 1856) than
for his own situation in Europe and for effecting a rapprochement with Russia while still maintaining the English alliance.
Had he felt stronger, had he been able, as Cowley suggested,
to induce England to make the war more 'popular' by widening
its aims so as to redraw the map of Europe, he might have

been ready to back Palmerston in his desire to inflict a more humiliating defeat on Russia. But England still clung to the 1815 settlement, while the war had already effected what looked like an irreparable breach between Russia and Austria, and so there was already opened up for Napoleon the greater freedom of diplomatic movement he so much desired. In these circumstances he could hasten the conclusion of peace without loss of prestige. In doing so he did not hesitate to intimate privately to the Tsar that, if Russia did not come to terms, he would 'appeal to the nationalities and particularly to the nation of Poland'. This pressure, together with his hints that, once peace was made, he would gladly come to an understanding with Russia, was effective, and in January 1856 the Tsar made known his readiness to accept the Allied peace terms which had already been the subject of prolonged negotiation.

The congress which terminated the war guaranteed the integrity of the Ottoman Empire, reaffirmed the closure of the Straits, neutralized the Black Sea and secured both Bessarabia and a considerable degree of autonomy for the Principalities. France's tangible gains were few, but the very fact that the congress was held in Paris and presided over by her Foreign Minister was a measure of her new prestige. In a few years her parvenu Emperor by his diplomacy and determination had restored her to the foremost rank among the great Powers. The French administration, for all the shortcomings of the military services, had stood the strain of war remarkably well. The country's financial strength had been demonstrated by the success of three war loans. The conclusion of peace had brought the Emperor renewed popularity at home, and the birth of the Prince Imperial before the congress ended appeared a happy omen for the stability and prosperity of the regime.

But the Congress of Paris left the European map substantially unaltered. Napoleon had had to abandon his plan of making the restoration of an independent Poland a *sine qua non* of the peace conditions to be imposed on Russia, and, although the Italian question had been ventilated at the congress, the territorial *status quo* in the Italian peninsula remained intact. His foreign minister for much of the time since 1848 had been the traditionalist Drouyn de Lhuys, who distrusted England, who held that France's superiority rested on her national unity, that everything that promoted the division of 'the great races' was useful to her, and whose triumph during the Crimean War had been to negotiate the alliance with Austria. Together with Austria, he had urged, Napoleon could be master of Europe and contain both 'ambitious Prussia' and 'revolutionary Italy'. This was not, however, the Napoleonic ideal for Europe. Drouyn de Lhuys was dropped before the war ended, and the Congress of Paris marked the end of one phase in Napoleon's foreign policy and the beginning of a new one in which the Emperor was to show himself at his most 'revolutionary'. The ally he wanted was not the one preferred by England, conservative Austria, but Russia, now a defeated power no longer so interested in maintaining the *status quo*. The new phase was one in which the Anglo-French alliance of the Crimean War would soon seem to have been, in Palmerston's phrase, 'but a summer season's partnership', for relations between the two countries rapidly deteriorated in consequence of the Orsini affair of 1858 and, in particular, of the new French naval programme, which led to a veritable invasion scare in England. It was the phase in which Napoleon appeared most clearly as a champion of nationalities, obliging the Sultan to recognize the independence of Montenegro (1858), facilitating the dynastic consolidation of Serbia, and personally directing the policy whereby the Roumanians of the Principalities circumvented the limitations placed upon them by the Treaty of Paris and achieved unity in 1861. But these successes were overshadowed by the much greater question of the liberation of Italy.

Of all foreign lands it was Italy, as we have seen, that lay nearest to Napoleon's heart. On grounds of sentiment as well as of revolutionary principle or ideology it irked him that two of her fairest northern provinces should still be ruled by the Austrians into whose hands he had nearly fallen in 1831. In 1853 the Austrian Ambassador, Hübner, had expressed his anxiety lest the Emperor 'essentially a Corsican, that is to say naturally harbouring resentment', should create difficulties for Austria 'by secretly supporting Sardinia and perhaps the demagogic party throughout the Peninsula'. In 1854 Cowley men-

Italy 1859–60

tioned that since the beginning of 'this Eastern Question', Napoleon had 'always had what he calls "his dreams" and that one of them was that Austria should give up her Italian provinces and receive the Principalities in exchange'. But this dream had not materialized: indeed by supporting Roumanian autonomy Napoleon himself made its realization impossible.

Nevertheless, at the end of 1855 he had asked the Sardinian Prime Minister, Cavour, to suggest what he could do for Piedmont and for Italy, and from then on that able man was in frequent touch with the Emperor. Napoleon's own schemes included the formation of a federation of Italian states to be presided over by the Pope, but there is no knowing for how long these schemes would 'like rabbits', in Palmerston's later phrase, have 'gone to earth', had it not been for a dramatic attempt on his life by an Italian patriot in January 1858, as he and the Empress were on the way to the Opera. The English-made bombs of Orsini, which caused many casualties, altered the whole chronology of the Italian question.

At first, by natural reaction, it looked as though the Orsini affair, temporarily if not permanently estranging France from England and Sardinia, both of whom sheltered some of the more revolutionary Italian exiles, would drive the Emperor into more conservative policies. But the strong pro-Italian group in his entourage strained every nerve to prevent this and to persuade their fatalistic master that here, paradoxically, was the opportunity indicated by destiny 'to do something' for Italy. The economic recession of 1857 and the continuance of opposition in the towns had caused him anxiety, and, if the not very reliable Prince Napoleon is to be believed, his cousin actually told him after the Orsini attempt that the new Empire and the Emperor personally needed fresh glory since the successes of the Crimea no longer sufficed. Thus, Napoleon was the more easily persuaded to change his course. Orsini was induced from his prison to write a moving appeal to the Emperor to act on behalf of Italian independence, and Napoleon allowed this to be published in the official *Moniteur universel*; at the same time the Imperial secretariat arranged for a similar 'political testament' of the patriot to be published under Cavour's auspices in Turin. In this way all could know that

Italian patriots looked to the Emperor to espouse their cause. While his government openly took a strong line with England and Sardinia for harbouring conspirators and refugees, he secretly prepared for action at Sardinia's side. In May, Cavour was delighted to receive a communication from Paris proposing a Franco-Sardinian alliance with a view to war against Austria, the formation of a kingdom of Upper Italy, and a marriage between Prince Napoleon and the Sardinian king's eldest daughter. Negotiations took place secretly through Cavour's private secretary and Napoleon's Italophil friend and doctor, Conneau, and in July, unknown even to his ministers, Napoleon arranged for Cavour to meet him at the watering place of Plombières. There, first in the Emperor's study and then in a phaeton driven through the neighbouring Vosges by Napoleon himself, the two men concerted a momentous plan which was to be confirmed with some modifications in a formal agreement in January 1859. French bankers, investors and engineers had already aided Sardinia economically. Now Napoleon consented to aid her in making Italy free from the Alps to the Adriatic and in replacing the old order by a federation of three or four Italian states—in the north Sardinia (enlarged to include Lombardy and Venetia after the Austrians had been expelled), in the middle a Central Italian kingdom and a reduced Papal State, and, undisturbed in the south, the Kingdom of the Two Sicilies. In return, the Emperor was to gain the satisfaction of a dynastic alliance by marrying his cousin, Prince Napoleon, to the daughter of Victor Emmanuel of Sardinia, and France was to receive Nice and Savoy.

It remained to prepare the ground and to find a *casus belli* against Austria. Napoleon dared not go to war without any continental ally, especially when his relations with England had so much deteriorated since the Crimean War. Negotiations were resumed with Russia, whose alliance he had long been seeking, but the Franco-Russian agreement of March 3, 1859, was a limited one. In return for an undertaking that, should war end with a congress, Napoleon and Cavour would support Russia's request for a revision of the Black Sea clauses of the Treaty of Paris, Russia undertook to keep troops on her

Austrian border and not to hinder their plans to expel Austria from Northern Italy. (It was incidentally a vivid example of Napoleon's opportunism that the neutralization of the Black Sea which he was now ready to abandon was the peace condition on which he had been most insistent in 1856.) Russia would thus help to contain Austria, but she was under no obligation to prevent any other German state, in particular Prussia, from coming to Austria's aid against France.

Here was the risk which was one of the factors which accounted for the Emperor's hesitations both before and during the coming war. For the step he was about to take was far more perilous than a distant war against Russia in alliance with England and Turkey. Then he was fighting with a strong ally an aggressive state which, itself afraid, aimed at upsetting the Near Eastern balance of power. Now he was about to embark on a blatantly aggressive war which, unjustified by any Austrian violation of treaties, was deliberately aimed at the overthrow of a settlement that treaties had consecrated, and in which his only ally was a small, albeit the most efficient Italian state. Apart from Russia, he faced the opposition of all the conservative forces and of all those who did not wish the peace of Europe to be disturbed by a new conflict; and this opposition was to be found not only abroad, but also in his own country— in the administration, in business circles and, still more passionately, in the Church. So the tireless zeal of Cavour in preparing for and urging his ally on to the fray vividly contrasted with the blowing hot and cold of Napoleon, whose regret, publicly expressed at his New Year's reception in 1859, that the relations between Paris and Vienna were not as good as he himself could wish, was widely but erroneously taken to allude to the Italian situation. Yet these fluctuations were probably calculated. Napoleon had crossed his Rubicon. The proposal now made for a European congress to settle the Italian question came not from him but from Russia and perhaps not on his prompting. When he agreed to it it was because, he told Prince Napoleon in March, he must make 'loud profession' of his moderation and of his desire for conciliation in order to divide his enemies and win over part of Europe to neutrality.

Austria would only go to a congress if Sardinia first agreed to disarm. On April 19 British and French pressure induced the reluctant Cavour to consent and it looked as though war was averted. But at this moment the Austrians overreached themselves in sending Sardinia an ultimatum which they rightly expected her to reject. Napoleon was to have his war; one of his great hours had come.

There had been overwhelming reasons to deter him from going to the Crimea, but now he intended to exercise his constitutional powers and test the belief he had voiced years before, that he had every military quality for the command of a great army. The Empress was made Regent and in May he was in Italy directing operations. Before the end of June the Franco-Sardinian forces had twice defeated the enemy, at Magenta and Solferino, names still commemorated in Parisian streets, and the Austrians had been driven from Lombardy. But these successes were due rather to the blunders of the Austrian command than to any brilliant generalship by Napoleon. His instructions for his field orders to be destroyed at the end of the campaign were sad recognition of his discovery that, when the test came, he had none of his uncle's military genius. The French losses were heavy, the Austrians reinforced could fall back on their strong fortresses in North-eastern Italy, the so-called Quadrilateral, and a long campaign still loomed ahead. Moreover, French clerical opinion was alarmed by the revolt in mid-June of the Romagna, the northern province of the Papal States, against papal government, and by the end of the month news came that Prussian forces were concentrating in the Rhineland. The Prussians feared that if he were victorious in Italy, Napoleon might rapidly turn against them in pursuit of his Rhenish ambitions. Napoleon, on the other hand, feared that Prussia might rally to Austria's support while he was still involved in Italy and that neither England nor Russia would come to his aid. He did not feel strong enough to face a war on two fronts unaided, and so, after only eight weeks' hostilities, he decided on a far more dramatic repetition of his policy at the end of the Crimean War, on bringing the war to a close as speedily as possible and effecting at least a temporary *rapprochement* with the enemy.

On July 11, to the general astonishment and to the rage and mortification of his Italian allies, he met the Austrian Emperor, Francis Joseph, at Villafranca and agreed to an armistice, the terms of which were later, on November 10, 1859, for the most part embodied in the Treaty of Zürich. Francis Joseph was to cede Lombardy to Napoleon, who would hand it over to Sardinia. Venetia was to remain under Austrian rule but to be member of a new Italian Confederation presided over by the Pope, the rulers of some of the lesser Central Italian states, who at the outset of the war had been expelled by their subjects, were to be reinstated, and the whole settlement was ultimately to be approved by a European congress.

A month later, back in Paris, the Emperor of the French received the congratulations of the Chambers and the Council of State, and he proceeded to review his victorious troops in the Place Vendôme with the three year old Prince Imperial dressed in the red and blue uniform of the Grenadiers sitting on his saddle-bow. The date chosen was the official birthday of Napoleon I. The popular applause was tremendous. The Second Empire had reached its apogee. But in reality this Italian victory was only half a victory militarily and politically. The weaknesses in the French army had again been exposed; Italy had not been freed from the Alps to the Adriatic; and in consequence France had not obtained Nice and Savoy. Thus the Italian question was far from being solved. Napoleon, who had not yet succeeded in extricating his troops from Rome where they had been since 1849, was in consequence to become still more deeply involved in the Italian imbroglio. And the clouds that gathered abroad soon cast their shadows at home.

Chapter Six

The 'New Course' in Politics

IN the 'silent years' from 1852 to 1860, when the political life of France was at its lowest ebb, there was much that could lead the Emperor to believe that his remedy of restrictive authoritarianism combined with strong doses of economic stimulus, military glory, and diplomatic prestige, had been effective, that opposition had been reduced to negligible proportions, and that he was succeeding, where his uncle had failed, in recreating harmony among Frenchmen and bringing the vast majority to accept without question the Napoleonic order of things. The opposition of the Liberal Catholics, for all their brilliance, was hardly to be feared, since they lacked popular backing and the support of the Pope. The activities of the Legitimists were diminished because their 'king', the Comte de Chambord, had enjoined them to abstain from politics. Many Orleanists, essentially a party of politicians, civil servants, business men and intellectuals without great popular following in the country, had entered Napoleon's service. The Republicans, decimated by exile and deportation, were weakened by the absence of some of their former leaders and by the refusal of others to take the oath of allegiance. Even the Parisian workers, who, like those in other big towns, at first had held aloof, had enthusiastically acclaimed the Emperor on his way to and from the Italian war and, with renewed prosperity, seemed to be drawing closer to the regime. In the meantime the country had in 1857 again gone quietly to the polls to choose a new Legislative Body. The government candidates, for the most part the same men who had sat in the previous Chamber, had polled almost the same number of votes as in 1852 and, although the opposition votes cast in certain towns, particularly Paris, caused the Emperor disquiet, the number of opposition deputies returned was still only a handful. The new Legislative Body looked like being as inoffensive as the old, little more than a glorified *Conseil Général*. Orsini's attempt on the Emperor's life, while it had been a dramatic reminder of the precariousness of the dynasty—the Prince Imperial was not yet two—and been followed by a severe but temporary tightening of authoritarian control, had increased his popularity, and the Italian war had enhanced it still further, except in Catholic and conservative circles. On his return to Paris Napoleon had felt strong enough to make a generous gesture and to amnesty as many as 1,800 political offenders.

The Italian war of 1859 and the Anglo-French commercial treaty of January 23, 1860, marked, however, a turning point in the policies of the regime. The treaty, as we have seen, roused the indignation and wrath of the protectionists, who felt they had been betrayed. The new policy in Italy, particularly the readiness, at first indicated in La Guéronnière's famous pamphlet of December 1859, *Le Pape et le Congrès*, of Napoleon to see the temporal sovereignty of the Papacy reduced, caused dismay and agitation amongst French Catholics, especially the numerous lower clergy and laymen who were avid readers of Louis Veuillot's vitriolic and influential paper, the Ultramontane *Univers*. The agitation was such that the government had to take repressive measures and also to suppress the *Univers*. Their firmness was rewarded. Despite the Pope's encyclical of January 19, 1860, which had called upon the bishops to 'influence their faithful to an unflinching defence of the Temporal Power', the agitation soon died down and Napoleon could note that the nation as a whole was unaffected. 'So long', it has been said, 'as worship was not interfered with, the Catholic masses refused to believe that the Church was in danger' and 'no further attempts of the sort were made under the Empire'. The acquiescence of the majority of Catholics no doubt made it easier for the Emperor to embark upon a definite change of policy towards the Church. If it would no longer co-operate, nor would he. He forbade the publication in France of Pius IX's famous encyclical *Quanta cura* condemning the errors of the modern world and of the Syllabus of Errors which accompanied it. He refused to consult the Pope before making further nominations of bishops. Obstacles were now put in the way of the religious orders, which hitherto had flourished and expanded so greatly, and after 1862 State schools were systematically encouraged in preference to those controlled by the clergy.

The increased tension between Church and State and the anger of the industrialists and other strong protectionists at his new free trade policy were no doubt among the reasons which led Napoleon to broaden the basis of his government and to initiate the slow and hesitant process whereby his authoritarian empire was eventually transformed into a liberal regime. But his decision was not a capitulation to irresistible public pressures. In fact there is much to be said for the view that Napoleon, who at the outset had spoken of an eventual return of liberty, now genuinely believed that the moment had come when, from a position still of great strength, he could make such a move, and that it was not uncongenial for him to do so. As Thiers acutely suggested at the time, there were other reasons, both practical and sentimental, which could help to explain the Emperor's decision. The fears and disorders engendered by the Second Republic were not comparable to those born of the great Revolution. An authoritarian regime was possible so long as fear of the 'reds' was dominant in society, but, after nine years, that fear no longer existed and 'the characteristic indocility of the century and of France' was beginning to reappear. Even the government men of the Legislative Body, some of whom had sat in the parliaments of the July Monarchy, inevitably, as time went on, fretted at being treated as dummies and longed for a greater share in debate and a greater control over an ever-mounting government expenditure. Moreover, as deputies became more critical and restive, ministers and deputies alike found it unsatisfactory that the exposition and defence of governmental policy in the Chambers should be left, as half a century earlier, to a civil servant, 'a poor little Counsellor of State'.

Thus, expediency and practical convenience alike led men such as Morny and Billault to favour the changes on which their master now decided. It was only prudent in the Emperor 'to forestall the day when concessions would no longer be voluntary'. Moreover, there was a strong reason of logic. In Thiers' words: 'it was impossible to continue the contrast of France giving liberty to all the world and refusing it for herself'; and again: 'to preach liberty, sword in hand, to the whole world, to tell the Pope, the King of Naples, the rulers of Tuscany and Modena, and the Emperor of Austria himself, that they were perishing or would perish for having refused sufficient liberty to their subjects, and to make us live under the institutions of the first Empire . . . without even the corrective of the Additional Act, this had become . . . almost ludicrous'. Finally, Thiers suggested that Napoleon's 'very strong affection for his son played its part in deciding him. Obviously he wanted to prepare the future for this child.'

Napoleon's momentous decision, which surprised many of the ministers themselves, was made known in a decree of November 24, 1860. The Chambers were now to be permitted to vote an address in reply to the annual message from the throne, their powers of debate were to be enlarged, the government's bills would henceforward be defended in the legislature by Ministers without portfolio, and permission was given for the debates in the Chambers to be published *in extenso*. This was the most important of a series of measures, which included decrees of January 1860 and July 1861 mitigating the severity of the press laws and a *Sénatus-Consulte* of December 31, 1861, extending parliamentary control over government expenditure. Even experts like the minister Fould had become alarmed at the way in which this had mounted without adequate safeguards, and Napoleon now approved the proposals of Fould that the budget should be voted section by section and not as hitherto *en bloc* for each ministry and that a vote of the Legislative Body should be required before the Emperor could open supplementary credits. It might have been supposed that these financial changes were of purely domestic concern, but Napoleon's own words of explanation, as reported by one of his ministers after a ministerial council, most revealingly indicate the all-pervading influence of foreign policy: 'I also wanted to destroy this notion which they pretend to hold abroad that my government is so absolute that I hold all the wealth of France in my hands, and that I can

dispose of it as I please even for my personal needs . . . This
is one of the main causes of the fear and the suspicion which
France causes abroad, because it is believed that suddenly,
without any previous discussion . . . I can secretly acquire huge
sums, for example to make military preparations.'

These political reforms meant that the insignificant Legislative Body of 1857 had, when it dispersed in 1863, become, as
Jules Ferry said, a parliamentary assembly. The sessions were
lengthened because of the exigencies of the debates on the
budget, the debates themselves became more animated, and the
five deputies of the Republican opposition, though they themselves were far from being a homogeneous group, systematically
criticized the authoritarian regime and demanded yet further
liberties. In a long debate in February 1861 concerning the
Roman question a Catholic amendment to the relevant part
of the address won as many as 91 votes. The Minister of the
Interior, Persigny, indignantly exploded: 'We shall meet again
in the elections!'

The elections of 1863 would indeed be a test of the popularity of the Emperor's new course and a significant indication
of his success in winning the support of the Left to compensate
for the falling away of the Right. They caused a political
excitement unknown since the *coup d'état* and stirred some
of the great parliamentarians of the past, men such as Thiers,
Berryer, and Montalembert to re-enter the lists. Although Persigny claimed that the results were a triumph, since the
government gained ground in the west, its supporters received
much the same number of votes as in 1852 and 1857, and no
purely clerical candidates were elected, he had to admit that
'for the first time for ten years a coalition has been formed
between the men whose views bind them to the previous
governments; in some places it has succeeded in taking the
voters by surprise'. In fact, as a prefect had written in 1862,
the electorate was 'no longer willing to be guided'. The
Emperor and his government were much dismayed: the opposition had polled double the number of votes they had received
in 1857 and thirty-two of their candidates were elected, seventeen Republicans and fifteen Monarchists or Catholics who sat
as 'independents'. Moreover, the department of the Seine had

chosen none but opposition candidates, eight Republicans and that experienced Orleanist, Thiers. Napoleon showed his displeasure by dismissing Persigny for not preparing for the elections with sufficient care. 'Your superior and lucid mind', he informed his old comrade, 'is worthless for administration'. He gave him a dukedom, but Persigny's ministerial days were done.

An opposition of 32 in a house of 282 deputies was small enough, but the disquieting thing was that the old parties had not been eliminated, that the Republicans had so much increased in strength, and that the hostility of the big towns, especially Paris, was more marked, despite all Napoleon's efforts to propitiate the workers.

In fact, Napoleon, for all the delusive appearances to the contrary during 'the silent years', had not succeeded in winning the whole-hearted allegiance of important sections of society and this failure became more apparent both because his embarrassments multiplied abroad and because parliament now had more freedom to express its discontent. When Persigny in a paradoxical way had said to Hübner in October 1853: 'The Emperor Napoleon has the support of the masses; Austria has that of the upper classes; give us the upper classes, we will give you the masses', he knew that there were certain élites whom the Empire had failed to rally. These included not only the Liberal Catholics, but many of the leading intellectuals of the Legitimist aristocracy and of the Orleanists, who had not forgiven Napoleon his confiscation of the property of the Orleans family in 1852 and who detested the man who had deprived them of a parliamentary system in which they played a dominant role. Moreover, in so far as the largely Orleanist bourgeoisie had accepted the regime, it was not only out of fear, but also in the hope of being able to exploit it in their own interests, since Napoleon, who had no sufficient élite of his own, must to a considerable extent rely upon them. Hence their anger at the free-trade treaty, hence the increasing pressure to obtain through parliament a control over policies which, to men with the narrow traditionalist outlook of the July Monarchy, appeared dangerously adventurous and extravagant. These 'liberals' were, in many ways, orthodox and conservative and they sought by capturing the regime from within to bend it to more orthodox and conservative courses.

The opposition of the Republicans, though less insidious, was more intransigent and disturbing. Nothing more vividly illustrated the truth of Napoleon's own assertion years before in his *Fragments historiques* that 'the origin of a government influences the whole of its existence' than his relationship with the party which ideologically was nearest to his own. Before 1848 Republicans and Bonapartists had often worked together, many of Louis Napoleon's personal friends and correspondents had been Republicans, and in his *Rêveries politiques* the regime he had dreamed of had been a kind of crowned Republic, which would have 'all the advantages of the Republic without its inconveniences'. In 1848 there had still been many workers and others who could cry in the same breath 'Vive la République! Vive Napoléon!' as though he were the incarnation of their Republican ideal. But thenceforward, determined to woo or outbid the bourgeoisie as a 'man of order', he had progressively severed his ties with the Republicans, allowing their leaders to be exiled and their party to be the main target of conservative repression. Finally, in the *coup d'état* and its aftermath he had himself completed the work of proscription and exile on a still more extensive and ruthless scale. Thereby he had made of his erstwhile friends irreconcilable enemies. For them he was the 'man of December', the man who was pilloried by Victor Hugo as 'Napoleon the Little' and who had won his way to power by perjury, bloodshed and wholesale repression. No wonder that, as the Empress said, he wore the Second of December like a shirt of Nessus; that it was a load which was always on his mind.

The opposition of the workers was obviously determined by the degree to which they were Republicans. Some undoubtedly had a strong allegiance to Republicanism, but there were many who were uncommitted or politically indifferent and it was these that Napoleon hoped to win. That many contemporaries regarded his social ideas as remarkably advanced is shown by Guizot's comment that his advent to power heralded the reign of Socialism. Napoleon himself in one of his best known *mots* claimed to be one:— 'the Empress is a Legitimist; Morny is an Orleanist; my cousin Napoleon is a Republican; I am a Socialist; only Persigny is a Bonapartist, and he is crazy'—and many historians since have described him as such. Yet it has been acutely remarked that Socialists themselves have never regarded him as one of their own.

Apart from his Saint-Simonian attitude to the development of national wealth, his claim to be regarded as a Socialist was based largely on *L'Extinction du Paupérisme*, which was archaic in its main conception, because, instead of considering the problem of poverty in the context of an increasingly industrialized society, he sought a solution in putting the workers back on the land. But though his 'socialism' may rest on slender foundations, he had a genuine if paternalistic concern for the well-being of ordinary Frenchmen and was full of schemes for the improvement of their lot, schemes for old-age pensions and accident insurance, provident societies and co-operative mining, for free litigation and burial for the poor, and even for compulsory State insurance. At Prince Napoleon's instance in 1862 he subsidized the visit of a workers' delegation to an exhibition in London, a visit which was to have far-reaching consequences, for the French delegates made contact with English trade-unionists and out of their agreement to keep in touch was born the first Workers' International, founded in London in 1864. In the same year 1864 he pressed through the Legislative Body a combination act, partly inspired by English practice and ideas, which legalized strikes, provided they were peaceful, and subsequently the Civil Code was modified to establish the equality of employer and employed before the law. Finally, in 1868 he permitted French workers to form unions with the result that the last two years of the Empire were notable for the rapid growth of workers' organizations especially in skilled occupations.

All these were measures which showed that the Emperor sought to stem the hostile currents revealed in the elections of 1863 and that, in J. M. Thompson's words, he 'never ceased to clutch the inviolable shade of social equality and justice which still eludes a less corrupt and prejudiced age'; but they would not achieve his goal. The mass of the workers was not to be won, for his approach was too paternalistic, real wages did not increase despite the economic dynamism of the regime, Republicanism continued to make headway, and many of those who were not Republican suspected government of any kind.

The elections of 1863 ensured that the new Legislative Body would be still more animated than its predecessor. But the great question in French politics after the reforms of 1860–1 was whether they were a beginning or an end, the beginning of a whole new evolution or merely a temporary gesture born of expediency. 'If it is an end', a young Republican deputy of talent, Emile Ollivier, one of 'the Five' elected in 1857, told Morny, 'you are lost; if it is a beginning, you are made (vous êtes fondés)'; and he had himself in a speech already indicated that, although he was a Republican, he would be ready to support the Emperor if he voluntarily assumed the courageous role of 'summoning a great people to liberty'. In Morny, who had presided over the Legislative Body with astuteness and charm since 1854, he found a sympathetic hearer who believed that it was essential that the Emperor should avoid the fate of Charles X and Louis Philippe by marching ahead of events and making concessions in time. In a note written soon after the elections and destined for Napoleon himself Morny expressed himself very frankly: 'The elections have left only two forces confronting one another: the Emperor and the democracy. The forces of democracy will grow continually; it is urgent to satisfy them if we do not want them to carry us away . . . It is time to do away with the abuses of nepotism . . . and to grant at once, if not entire political liberty, at least civil liberty. It is urgent that the Emperor should cease to spring surprises and to leave his advisers in complete ignorance of his foreign policy.'

But Morny's advice, which he continued to press on Napoleon until his death in 1865, went unheeded, and his plans for a ministry, headed by Ollivier and himself, to put through such a programme of further reform came to nothing. Even had the Emperor been willing to sponsor it, there was as yet no sufficient following on which a liberal ministry could be based.

The drawbacks of a system in which there was no ministerial solidarity, no coherent programme on which the ministers and their master were all agreed, became all the more evident as

Napoleon's health declined and his policies abroad in Italy, Poland, Mexico, and Germany met with rebuffs. Already in 1859, Prince Napoleon, always a candid critic and then Minister for Algeria, had told the Emperor that the worst features of his government lay in 'the different views held by those directing it. The greater the degree in which authority is strong and concentrated in the hands of the Emperor, the more indispensable is unity among those who serve him'. In 1862 other ministers had argued strongly in favour of the principle of solidarity and a greater unity in the direction of foreign affairs. But Napoleon, jealous of his authority, had refused to make more than a verbal admission that the principle had a *de facto* validity. Moreover, if Morny (whose death in 1865 was a tragedy, since he was nearer to being a statesman than any of the other protagonists of the Empire) was a liberal, others in Napoleon's entourage regarded the 'new course' with horror and were strongly opposed to further concessions. In such circumstances, the Emperor, whom Hübner had long before described as liking to have a foot in both camps, characteristically pursued a see-saw policy, oscillating like the Directors at the end of the eighteenth century, now to the Left and now to the Right.

For the time being, apart from social legislation and the more secular education programme presided over by the new and able education minister, the anti-clerical Victor Duruy, whose merits Napoleon had discovered when he enlisted his aid in the preparation of his own *Vie de César*, the swing was to the Right. Parliamentary control over supplementary credits was stultified by a new degree enabling the government to rectify the budget, and the Ministers without Portfolio who defended government policy in the Chamber were superseded by a single Minister of State. After Billault's death in October 1863, this post was given to the authoritarian and powerful Eugène Rouher, whom men soon dubbed 'Vice Emperor' while wits called the government the 'Rouhernement', since he was the sole interpreter of government policy in Parliament and the Emperor appeared increasingly to lean upon him. Unfortunately Rouher, though a tremendous worker and highly competent debater, was a man without ideas. As Michel Chevalier said, he was 'the Atlas of the regime, but the advocate who pleads its cause rather than the statesman who directs it'.

Inevitably the liberals in the Legislative Body were dissatisfied and began to form a centre group or 'Third Party'. They were men who were ready to accept the dynasty, as opposed to the intransigent Republicans on the Left and the avowed Legitimists on the Right, but who pressed for the concession of 'the necessary freedoms'. It was Thiers who, in a celebrated speech in January 1864, expounded what these were: individual liberty, liberty of the press, freedom of elections and ministerial responsibility. But Rouher's reply was a peremptory refusal: 'The Emperor has not restored the throne in order to abandon government, to deliver authority to the manoeuvres of parliamentary government and, as in 1848, to put back the pyramid on its summit'. This rejection had the effect of increasing the numbers and vigour of the 'Third Party', who were joined by 'liberal' supporters of the government as well as by conservatives and Catholics. In March 1866 a liberal Orleanist, Buffet, moved an amendment to the address, which renewed Thiers' appeal of two years earlier: 'France', it ran, 'firmly attached to the dynasty which guarantees order, is no less attached to liberty which she believes to be necessary for the fulfilment of her destinies. Thus the Legislative Body believes that it is interpreting public opinion by bringing to the foot of the throne the wish that Your Majesty should give to the great act of 1860 the development that befits it. The experience of five years appears to have demonstrated its suitability and timeliness'. The amendment was supported by 60 votes—the opposition of 1863 had almost doubled.

Although Napoleon made a kind of half-gesture of offering Ollivier a ministerial post, which he refused, it was ten months before he answered the appeal, and even then his decision, abruptly announced in a letter to the *Moniteur* on January 19, 1867, might well not have been made, but for the blow to France's prestige and international position inflicted by Prussia's victory over Austria at Sadowa in July 1866. Nevertheless, the letter of January 19 marked a notable step forward, and, since it came at a time when no such move was expected, Napoleon could again appear to have retained the initiative in

'giving to the institutions of the Empire', as he said, 'all the
development of which they are susceptible and to public
liberties a new extension without compromising the power
conferred upon me by the nation'. The address in reply to the
message from the throne was done away with; instead deputies
were allowed to interpellate the Government and ministers
could take part in debates, the fresh importance of which
would incidentally soon be signalized by the reappearance of
the orator's tribune. This enhancement of the role of parliament
was to be accompanied by legislation recognizing and regulat-
ing the right of meeting and relaxing the government's control
of the press.

These measures marked a considerable stage further in the
liberalization of the regime, but they did not mean the restoration of parliamentary government, for the ministers remained
responsible only to the Emperor, who was still unwilling to
form them into a team and admit the principle of ministerial
solidarity. Moreover, the good impression made by Napoleon's
letter of January 19, 1867, was largely undone by the fact that
he did not change his men as well as his measures and by the
slowness with which the legislation on civil liberties was introduced. When men read that Rouher was to have still more
power, adding the Ministry of Finance to the post of Minister
of State, and that Baroche and others were still in office, they
said, so Prince Napoleon reported to the Emperor: ' "It is not
seriously meant." M. Thiers exclaimed, "It is a take in; but
we shall know how to profit by it." ' As the Prince reminded
his cousin: 'our Uncle in 1815 chose the support of Benjamin
Constant, [and] Sismondi, and appointed Carnot, the member
of the Committee of Public Safety, to be Minister of the
Interior. What confidence will be inspired by the words of a
Minister [Rouher] who can be led to praise that which a year
ago he condemned as seditious?'

The Emperor's lame reply indicated a further weakness of
his system of government. With one exception, Pinard, the new
Minister of the Interior, he did not bring in new men because
he had none on whom he could rely. The able young men were
attracted not to the service of an ageing sovereign, who still
treated his ministers as clerks, but to the Liberal and Repub-

lican groups who were increasingly the driving forces in parliament. If Napoleon did not wish to deliver himself over to old parliamentary hands like Thiers—and in a remark of rare candour he said that he had begun with the old men of the Rue de Poitiers (the headquarters of the 'Party of Order' in 1848) and was determined not to end with young ones of the same sort—he had to fall back again on Rouher and his fellows. Indeed, it was Rouher who contributed to Napoleon's hesitations over the promised press law. This meant that the new bill was not presented to the Chambers for several months and that it was not until May 11, 1868, that it became law. In consequence, a radical measure, which 'might well have been made to look . . . like a generous gift from the emperor', since it did away both with the preliminary authorization required to found a paper and with the system of warning, suspension, and suppression, was robbed of all its good effect. Its handling was, in the words of a recent English historian of the press of that time in France, 'a clear example of the muddle and indecision which reigned in government circles during the last years of the Empire, and of the emperor's pathetic failure to make the most of a difficult but by no means hopeless situation'.

As it turned out, the new press law immensely increased the power of all the forces of opposition. But it was to require another general election and fresh setbacks abroad before Napoleon was induced to take a further step towards the 'crowning of the edifice' and to adopt men of a new kind as well as new measures. A fatal blunder in foreign policy would decree that that step should be his last.

Chapter Seven

Foreign Policy: The Years of
Frustration

HAD Napoleon III died in the autumn of 1859 or the early summer of 1860 historians might well have accounted him the most successful of all France's rulers in the nineteenth century. Yet their verdict would scarcely have been unqualified. Was his last great venture in Italy really a success?

It has been argued that Napoleon at bottom favoured a bolder policy in Italy than might appear and that he actually wished for a unification of the peninsula which was in accordance both with the Napoleonic ideas and his own cherished principle of nationality. Yet the preponderating evidence suggests that unification was far from being his true aim, that he no more than Lord John Russell thought of it as a real or desirable possibility, and that in his handling of the Italian question he showed himself but an unskilled magician, conjuring up forces whose power he had underestimated and which he was unable to control.

There is little doubt that his real aim was revealed at Plombières and that he wished not merely to undo the treaties of 1815 by liberating Italy from Austrian rule and acquiring Nice and Savoy, but also to achieve in a new way the old French ambition of making French influence predominant in the peninsula. The confederation of Italian states envisaged in the Franco-Sardinian agreement of 1859 would, he had told Walewski, 'provide France with powerful allies who will owe her everything and depend only on her for their existence'. Unification, on the other hand, would, he himself admitted, 'create difficulties in France because of the Roman question' and because 'France would not see with pleasure the rise on

her flank of a great nation which might diminish her pre-
ponderance'.

Villafranca in fact made the achievement of the satellite
confederation of Napoleon's dreams impossible. Napoleon and
Francis Joseph might agree upon a settlement of Italy which
would restore the Central Italian rulers, establish a confederation, and be ratified by a congress, but the Treaty of Zürich
of November 10, 1859, which confirmed their agreement, was
virtually a dead letter from the moment it was signed, for it
took no account of the strength of Italian nationalism or the
astuteness of Cavour, and already Napoleon III was beginning
to shift his ground and change his policies.

After Villafranca the focus of interest rapidly moved from
Northern to Central Italy. Almost certainly Napoleon had been
taken by surprise by the revolutions which had occurred in the
Central Italian duchies and in the Romagna and which were
to jeopardize his plans for an Italian confederation. Yet he
himself, in his desire to rouse the enthusiasm of the Italians
for the war against Austria, had encouraged this movement by
issuing a proclamation to 'the Italians' after his victory at
Magenta, urging them to flock to the standard of Victor
Emmanuel, and telling them that, the French army placing no
obstacle in the way of the free demonstration of their legitimate
wishes, they would become 'free citizens of a great country'.
The proclamation might seem militarily expedient and echo
those issued by General Bonaparte after his entry into Milan
in 1796, but it was of very dubious political wisdom, unless he
were sure of complete success in the field.

Whether, in view of this attitude, the provision in the subsequent armistice that the former rulers of the Central Italian
states should be reinstated was a mere sop to Austria, and
whether Napoleon from the first disbelieved in the possibility
of its fulfilment, we do not know, but it was soon clear that
such a restoration could be accomplished only by force. Austria
after her recent defeats was in no position to use force unaided,
Sardinia was not committed, and Napoleon likewise had carefully avoided any obligation to employ French troops for such
a purpose. The use of force to reimpose the rule of petty
sovereigns whom he had no cause to love—at Plombières he

had referred to the Duke of Modena as the scapegoat of despotism—would have meant a sudden swing to a policy that would have been both unpopular and embarrassing, and he had already had embarrassment enough as a result of restoring the Pope to Rome. It would have been conceivable only had he been determined to alter his entire course, adopt a thorough-going conservative policy, and whole-heartedly embrace an Austrian alliance, as Drouyn de Lhuys had wished him to do during the Crimean War. That he should seriously contemplate such a change, and in Italy of all places, was indeed unlikely. There would be no serious pursuit of an Austrian alliance until Drouyn de Lhuys was back in office and the Polish crisis of 1863 once again suggested its expediency. It was apparent that the fate of Italy's fallen rulers was sealed and that they had no effective champion.

Meanwhile, however, Piedmontese propaganda had been active in stimulating the insurgent inhabitants of the Central Italian states to demand annexation to Sardinia and their provisional governments to adopt Sardinian institutions and choose a Sardinian as regent. The question was whether Napoleon would permit such an annexation and aggrandize-ment of Sardinia or whether he would still attempt to secure the creation of the separate Central Italian state he had originally contemplated. The resolution of this problem in-volved a complete re-orientation of his policy. The policy of Villafranca and Zürich was jettisoned, for the Emperor per-ceived that it was unworkable and that by discarding it he might after all secure one of his chief objectives. The agree-ment of Plombières had provided for the cession of Nice and Savoy to France in compensation for the aggrandizement of Sardinia to a kingdom 'of about eleven million inhabitants'. No doubt the agreement originally envisaged that this aggrand-izement would come about through the incorporation under Victor Emmanuel's rule of Venetia as well as Lombardy, but Venetia had not been specified and Napoleon now saw no objection to Sardinia's expansion southward instead of east-ward, provided he could obtain his price. For all his successes in war and diplomacy he had not so far gained for France an inch of territory. Now that he could not attain all his objectives in Italy, possession of Nice and Savoy would be worth much more than an artificial Central Italian state, which, as his own part in promoting Roumanian unity could well remind him, might be most difficult to maintain if its people were bent on union with Sardinia.

The new policy was dramatically heralded by the publication on December 22, 1859, of an anonymous pamphlet, not written by the Emperor but fully approved by him, entitled *Le Pape et le Congrès*.* In this the author, La Guéronnière, who professed himself a sincere Catholic, pointed out that, while some temporal power was needful for the Pope's spiritual authority, it should be strictly limited in extent: 'The smaller the territory, the greater the sovereign . . . The city of Rome is all that really matters.' This publication, which caused fury and consternation in the Vatican and among French Catholics, was a clear intimation that Napoleon, who, as long before as Christmas Day, 1848, had spoken privately of his desire 'to augment the spiritual by decreasing the temporal power of the Pope', had both abandoned the former rulers and would not lift a finger to help the Pope to recover control of the Romagna. Catholic Austria demanded that he should repudiate the arguments of the pamphlet and, when he refused, rejected the congress, so this proposal whereby the Powers might still have had a say in the shaping of Italy, in turn came to nothing. The way was open for further revolutions.

The Pope indignantly repudiated the idea of surrendering any part of his dominions, which, he claimed, belonged 'to all Catholics', but Napoleon held firmly to his new course. Already, when Walewski, his pro-Catholic foreign minister, had resigned on January 4, 1860, he had replaced him by the more liberal and capable Thouvenel. On January 23 he concluded the commercial treaty with England, which was designed to inaugurate his new economic policy and which might, it was hoped, bring about a much needed improvement in Anglo-French relations generally. Meanwhile, the return of Cavour to power a few days earlier enabled negotiations with Sardinia to be pressed ahead, for both sides were eager to secure their gains. In return for Napoleon's agreement to accept the results of plebiscites to

* See above, p. 85.

be held in Central Italy on the question of annexation to Sardinia, Cavour reluctantly acceded to Napoleon's demand for Nice and Savoy, provided that their union with France should also be subject to a plebiscite. Agreement was reached in March. The popular votes took place in March and April and recorded immense majorities in favour of Sardinia on the one hand and France on the other.

Thus the ten months since Villafranca had seen remarkable developments: the enunciation by Napoleon of a highly modern doctrine of the temporal power of the Papacy, the resurrection by Cavour of the principle of self-determination proclaimed by the French Constituent Assembly in 1791, but hardly applied so far in the nineteenth century, and the consequent transfer of considerable populations. Napoleon by diplomacy had after all acquired Nice and Savoy, thus dealing a decisive blow to the settlement of 1815. These territories were henceforward to be integral parts of France, and Italy was still divided, although into only four very unequal areas.

But the Italian Confederation had come to nothing and, instead of being regarded with general affection and gratitude by Italians, Napoleon was still unpopular in the north for failing to expel Austria and execrated in Rome for his readiness to sacrifice the Papal States. Moreover, his permanent gain of Nice and Savoy had cost him dear, for it had caused anxiety and suspicion among all France's neighbours. Napoleon represented it as 'a geographic necessity for the safety of the French border' and there is no doubt that this was a genuine motive for the annexation, but it awakened fears that it was but the beginning of a policy of aggrandizement based on the revolutionary doctrine of natural frontiers. Above all, it undid much of the good effect of the treaty of commerce with England. Napoleon's apparent duplicity—for he had earlier disclaimed any intention to ask for territorial gain for France—shocked English opinion from the Queen downwards; the annexation of Nice and Savoy played much the same part in the history of Anglo-French relations during the Second Empire as had the affair of the Spanish Marriages during the July Monarchy. On his side, Napoleon was so irritated and surprised by the public attacks on him in England that he allowed a rare 'upsurge of ill-humour' to get the better of him and publicly berated the British Ambassador at a concert at the Tuileries. The two countries did not come to the war that some at the time freely talked of, but the cordiality of the mid-'fifties was never to be restored, despite Napoleon's persistent efforts in 1860 and 1861 to repair the damage. After England had administered fresh rebuffs during the Polish crisis of 1863 it would be Napoleon's turn to be unco-operative.

Meanwhile, the plebiscites of the spring of 1860 had not ended the 'Italian question'. They had for the time being settled the Central Italian problem; there remained, however, Rome and also the South, uneasily quiescent under reactionary Bourbon rule.

The state of Franco-Papal relations made it more than ever an anomaly that Napoleon should keep in Rome French troops to defend a Pontiff who still refused to reform his government; but, in view of French Catholic opinion, strongly championed by the Empress, he could not afford to withdraw unless other arrangements were made for the security of the Pope and his dominions. The Papal Government, who rejected all Napoleon's schemes for their protection, eventually set about levying their own Catholic volunteers under the command of the French General Lamoricière, a former proscript of 1851, whose appointment Mgr. de Mérode delightedly described as 'a little slap for the Emperor'. This force seemed adequate to defend what was left of the Papal States, and in May, 1860, a convention was concluded whereby the French garrison should evacuate Rome at the end of three months.

Unfortunately for Napoleon, on the very day this convention was signed Garibaldi landed in Sicily. The Italian question was re-opened and the Roman question was to be given a further twist. Ten months earlier Lord John Russell had written: 'I dare say the dreamers wish to unite Naples and Sicily and make a kingdom of the whole of Italy, but that is wild and foolish.' Now, once Garibaldi was master of Sicily, unless the Great Powers and, in particular, Napoleon, intervened to prevent it, it looked as though the dreamers would have their way. As recently as March, Thouvenel had reminded the French Minister in Naples that the traditions and interests of French policy did not accord with the formation of a unitary state in the peninsula; yet Napoleon, though he hesitated greatly, took no decisive step to maintain these traditions and interests. He did indeed make somewhat dubious efforts at mediation and supported a proposal for Anglo-French naval intervention to prevent Garibaldi from crossing the Straits of Messina, but when the former came to nothing and the latter was rejected by England, he was resolved not to act alone. The man who had already refused to fight for reactionary Italian princes could hardly take up arms for the Bourbon monarch who was the most unpopular of them all. He could hardly obstruct the principle of self-determination in Southern Italy when he had so recently endorsed it in Emilia and Savoy. A revolutionary at heart, he still had a lurking sympathy for Italian national aspirations and this was increased by the obvious disapproval of the conservative powers. Moreover, it is probable that he was anxious not to fall further out of step with England, the other chief naval power in the Mediterranean, whose policy hitherto in the Italian question had, with some qualifications, been one of benevolent neutrality. So Napoleon, too, adopted a policy of non-intervention and in a remarkable letter to Persigny, communicated to the press in July, declared that he wished Italy to be 'pacified no matter how, provided I can get out of Rome without compromising the safety of the Pope and that there is no foreign intervention'.

In consequence, there was no external obstacle to Garibaldi's crossing to the mainland and threatening Naples itself. But Garibaldi was a Republican in sympathy and neither Cavour nor Napoleon was eager for Republican principles to be implanted in Southern Italy. Once again it rested with the Emperor to bless or veto Sardinian aggrandizement, which this time would mean Italian unification under the House of Savoy. Already in July he had given his approval to a scheme of Cavour's whereby Sardinia would counter Garibaldi and lead the movement for unification. When at the end of August Cavour's emissaries unfolded to Napoleon their master's plan to provoke insurrection in the Papal States, disarm the Garibaldians, and confiscate their victory in order to preserve 'the national and monarchical character of the Italian movement', the Emperor, who had already been willing to provide Sardinia with the latest French rifles, bade them act, but act quickly. Soon after, Napoleon departed to Algeria for a while as though to emphasize his new detachment from the Italian imbroglio. The way was thus clear for the Italian nationalists north and south of Rome. The last Neapolitan stronghold on the mainland fell in February 1861. Meanwhile Cavour and his agents had incorporated Umbria and the Marches in the Kingdom of Piedmont. Early in 1861, the first Italian parliament met in Turin, and in March Victor Emmanuel was proclaimed King of Italy.

But Napoleon III could not yet be detached from Rome. In the new crisis after Garibaldi's landing in Sicily Catholic opinion had required that the French troops should not after all be withdrawn in August 1860, and after Lamoricière's men had been routed at Castelfidardo in September it was still more difficult to take them away. Their occupation of Rome, which he now admitted to have been the one step in Italy he really regretted, had lasted eleven years. It was to be another three before it temporarily ceased. In June 1861 negotiations between Cavour and the Papacy, which would have permitted French withdrawal, were ended by Cavour's sudden death. At much the same time, two epileptic attacks suffered by Pius IX, together with the belief that the Pope had issued a secret brief to certain cardinals enjoining them, if he died, to elect a successor without waiting for a full conclave, altered the situation and led Napoleon for a while to wish to keep the garrison in Rome in order to be able to threaten its withdrawal should an election be held before the French and other liberal cardinals could arrive in Rome. Later, in 1862, after it seemed that Pius had no intention of dying, an arrangement projected by Thouvenel with the Italian Government was frustrated by the Empress who helped to bring about his fall and the return of the Catholic Drouyn de Lhuys to the Ministry of Foreign Affairs. It was not until 1864 that a Convention was at last concluded, in accordance with which, in return for an Italian undertaking to respect and defend the Papal territory, the French troops were to withdraw in 1866. Then at long last, on

December 12 of that year, Napoleon's men were evacuated. But not for long. In 1867 Garibaldi and, in reaction to him, the French Catholics were again fatefully to intervene. Napoleon was to find that the chain, which as a political novice he had forged with such insouciance in 1849, was 'to drag at his ankles to the end'.

In 1861, however, the year in which the Kingdom of Italy was established largely as a result of his complaisance, Napoleon, who had so recently modified the 1815 settlement and successfully patronized the subversive principle of nationality, could still appear to contemporaries the most powerful sovereign in Europe. He might hope to have recovered Italian goodwill by his attitude to unification in 1860 and to have secured in the new state if not a satellite at least a potential ally. He had avoided any further unpopular military commitment, and the failure of the three 'Northern courts' to reconstitute the Holy Alliance in face of the Italian question had removed the danger of 'foreign intervention'. Moreover, now that so many old ties were dissolved, he might seem freer than ever to manoeuvre as he pleased and to substitute his own system for that of 1815.

But this hegemony was not to last and any further redrawing of the map of Europe was not to be at his behest. We can only glimpse the system which he might have sought to develop had he been strong enough to impose his will: one in which the principle of nationalities would have received further consecration and in which the nation states would look to him as their ally or their patron and resolve their difficulties by means of congresses when the Emperor chose to summon them; one in which France herself would be the prime mover in a new age of Saint-Simonian prosperity, which would enable all those who traded and did business with her to benefit from her credit, her 'Latin' monetary system, her low tariffs and constantly improving communications. But such Napoleonic ideas in modern dress were to have no chance of application. So far from reordering Europe at his wish he was unable to secure even for France herself any further territorial and economic satisfaction on her eastern frontier.

Now that the Italian question was largely resolved, the centre of interest in Europe after 1861 tended to shift north of the Alps. The years 1863 to 1866 were dominated by three successive crises, in Poland, in Schleswig-Holstein, and in Germany proper, each of which had the effect directly or indirectly of weakening Napoleon's position.

The cause of Poland, a country long linked with France by ties of history and sentiment, was almost the only one which could rouse the sympathies of Frenchmen of every creed and party. For Louis Napoleon, who had been tempted to fight for the Polish insurgents in 1831, who had befriended their refugees, and who had numbered some of them among his adherents before 1848, Poland held second place only to Italy in his affections. During the Crimean War he had made repeated efforts to 'do something' for the Poles. An anonymous pamphlet sponsored by him had suggested the creation of a Prusso-Polish Kingdom at Russia's expense; in negotiations with Austria he had urged the need to grant the Poles in Russia a measure of independence by reconstituting his uncle's Grand Duchy of Warsaw. But Austria had refused to discuss Poland, and England had turned down his suggestion that the reconstitution of the 'Congress' Kingdom of Poland, abolished by Russia after the Polish revolt of 1831, should be one of the terms of the Treaty of Paris in 1856. So the Polish question remained unsolved and in January 1863 the Poles in Russia were driven by conscriptive measures to fresh revolt.

As Russia was his chief ally on the continent, this turn of affairs was most embarrassing to Napoleon. After the Crimean War he had done his best to urge the Tsar to conciliate the Poles, and at Stuttgart in 1857 he had warned him that the only obstacle to good Franco-Russian relations was the 'delicate' question of Poland. But Alexander's concessions to Poland misfired and, when revolt came, French public opinion, like British, at once manifested itself strongly on behalf of the rebels and required that something should be done. The fact that 1863 was an election year in France made it all the more difficult for the Emperor, who had been among the bitter critics of Louis Philippe's indifference to the Poles, to take no action.

But, already involved in Mexico,* and mindful, no doubt, that it had taken the combined efforts of France, Great Britain, Sardinia and Turkey to bring Russia to her knees in 1855–6, he dared not act alone. In April, he told one of his advisers that 'he had not closed his eyes for four nights, thinking of the wrongs of Poland and he, a Napoleon, unable to redress them'.

An attempt was made first to make Prussia the scapegoat because, fearing revolt in Prussian Poland, she had concluded a military convention with Russia, and then, since England would not co-operate, to reconstitute the Crimean War coalition of Great Britain, France, and Austria, and even to realize again Drouyn de Lhuys's old dream, favoured by the Empress, of an alliance with Austria. But Britain was preoccupied by the American Civil War, and Palmerston, though ready enough to use strong language because he wrongly believed that Russia would give way to diplomatic threats, was not prepared to back those threats by force; while Austria, afraid of imperilling her Polish province of Galicia, refused the proffered alliance and was more than ever lukewarm. So, although, as in the first year of the Crimean War, Napoleon entertained schemes for an expedition to the Baltic and received an offer of alliance from Charles XV of Sweden, such projects never got far. In July the British Government informed him that, whatever sympathy the public might feel for Poland, 'it would not induce the country to go to war with Russia'. From this position they were not to be moved and, as the French public, too, for all its desire to help the Poles, did not want war, it is doubtful whether the Emperor did so either. His last resort was to revive the expedient which had always been dear to him and to propose on November 4 a European congress. This, he suggested, would 'not only regulate the fate of Poland, but would substitute for the treaties of 1815, now in decay, new stipulations apt to ensure the peace of the world. Do we have to choose merely between silence and war? Let us not wait until irresistible events suddenly disturb our judgment and drive us, against our will, in opposite directions.' Unfortunately the Powers trusted him too little to listen to this appeal from the man of whom an American historian was to write that 'in

* See below, p. 137.

1863 he was perhaps the last genuine European who stood in a place of authority, a successor to Metternich, a precursor of Woodrow Wilson'. The Tsar would certainly have refused to attend such a gathering: but Britain, fearing fresh complications and above all the reopening of the Eastern Question, gratuitously anticipated him in rejecting it and did so 'in terms bordering on discourtesy', which caused Napoleon profound irritation.

The Polish crisis was thus a sorry affair for both the Western Powers. Rather than follow in the footsteps of Louis Philippe, Napoleon had, as he himself admitted, been prepared to sacrifice his friendship with Russia. But there had been no kind of gain to offset the sacrifice. France and Britain, as he later said, had received 'a big slap in the face' from Russia, who could not afford the fresh humiliation of surrender to the Poles at the bidding of the Western Powers. She had called their diplomatic bluff and firmly rejected all their protests and representations on behalf of the Poles. The Poles themselves were ruthlessly repressed, their lot made worse rather than better by the fruitless representations of England and France. Austria had proved a broken reed. The *coup de grâce* was given to the Anglo-French alliance, which was now, as a British Cabinet minister said, 'put in the lumber room', and Russia would henceforward sympathize with Napoleon's new and formidable rival, Prussia, rather than with France. Moreover, Napoleon's prestige had suffered at home as well as abroad. At the end of the year Baron Beyens, the Belgian Minister in Paris, noted that 'a vague feeling of fear' pervaded the situation in France: 'Almost by instinct they sense that they are on the threshold of great unknown events, and on every side I hear repeated: "If we are not at 1847, we are at least at 1845".'

Great and 'irresistible events' were soon to follow in Germany. The first was the recurrence of the dispute between Denmark and the German Confederation over the duchies of Schleswig and Holstein. Both had long been attached to the Danish crown, but Holstein was also a member of the German Confederation, and its inhabitants, as well as the southern Schleswigers, were German-speaking. In 1848-9 conflict had broken out as a result of a Danish attempt to incorporate

Schleswig into Denmark, but German nationalist aspirations to obtain full possession of both duchies had been frustrated by the intervention of the Great Powers and the resulting Treaty of London of 1852 had upheld the Danish connexion. This Treaty had, however, never been accepted by the German Diet and when in 1863 a new Danish king again attempted to unite Schleswig with his Danish dominions there was an immediate German outcry. Denmark rejected a German ultimatum and in consequence soon found herself at war with Prussia and Austria who had jointly assumed the leadership of the German cause.

Britain, the power most deeply concerned, was eager to protect Denmark and uphold the Treaty of London, yet she could not act alone, for she had no army to speak of. Napoleon, however, smarting from the rebuffs he had so recently received at her hands, was in no mind to come to her relief. Moreover, the Danish war was one which aroused the enthusiasm of all Germans. It would have been difficult for the Emperor, the foremost champion of nationalities, to oppose a national cause of this kind, and dangerous for him to embark upon a war against a nation of 40 millions. Thus, although he and his ministers characteristically threw out hints that they might reconsider their position if they could be sure of compensation in the Rhineland, in the end they took no positive action on behalf of the Danes. To us, who know how the formidable Prussian Minister-President Count Otto von Bismarck, called to power in 1862, was to profit by the Western Powers' supineness to build up Prussian strength in Germany, it may seem that a great opportunity was lost of their presenting a common front, which 'would have sufficed to maintain for many years peace and the respect for treaties'. There is no doubt, however, that, from the point of view of France's immediate interests, Napoleon was wise not to intervene. France's opportunity to assert herself with effect in the German question would be when the German powers fell out and not when they were united. Meanwhile the Danes, left to themselves, were easily defeated and obliged in August 1864 to surrender Schleswig and Holstein to Austria and Prussia. But the question of what to do with the spoils soon caused acute tension between the two victors and this was only temporarily relieved by the Convention of Gastein whereby Bismarck cynically 'papered over the cracks' on August 14, 1865.

The establishment of the German Confederation comprising thirty-nine states had been an integral part of the 1815 settlement, but the Confederation had proved a cumbrous and ineffective organism which the revolutionaries of 1848 had vainly attempted to supersede. The questions of German nationalism and German unity had both been posed in 1848–9, but they had not been resolved, and the main consequence of the upheavals of those years had been to accentuate the rivalry of the two leading powers, Prussia and Austria. Hitherto, all Austro-Prussian negotiations concerning Germany or Italy had been fruitless because Prussia's price for her support was the leadership in Germany which Francis Joseph was determined not to concede. Now, weary of this stalemate and encouraged by his reading of the European situation, Bismarck prepared to bring the issue to a head by war. The German question proper would confront Napoleon with some of the most fateful decisions of his career.

Unfortunately for France the man who was to be called upon to face the problems raised by Prussian ambition was no longer the physically active and alert Napoleon of the 'fifties. For some years now he had ceased to take the regular riding and walking exercise which had helped to keep him fit. He was, like his uncle, growing stout, and, unlike him, exhausted by various excesses, tended increasingly to let his natural disposition to indolence and aversion to the details of business get the better of him. Worst of all, in July 1865, his physician had diagnosed a serious ailment, a stone in the bladder. In spite of the fact that this was to cause him excruciating but intermittent pain he refused to be operated upon and insisted on his illness being kept a secret. This stoicism shortened his life, and his general physical deterioration meant that, while his intelligence and judgment were unimpaired, his will-power had been weakened. More than ever subjected to pressures of one kind or another, not least from the Empress, who had shown an increasing disposition to interfere in politics since the revival of the Roman question in 1859, he was in consequence more than ever hesitant and fluctuating in the pursuit of his ends.

Although his schooling at Augsburg and other connexions no doubt gave him a certain sympathy for the Southern German States, Napoleon seems never to have been emotionally stirred by the cause of German nationality in the way in which he was stirred by the causes of Italy and Poland. As Prince President, apart from showing his hostility to Schwarzenberg's schemes for Austrian aggrandizement, he had in November 1851 declared the need for France to remain strictly aloof from the Confederation's efforts at internal reorganization. This disinterestedness had not prevented his government from making soundings intermittently throughout the fifties and early sixties concerning the possibility of rectifying France's German frontier. No doubt Napoleon was aware of the advantages of a rectification which would not only further breach the Vienna settlement but also strengthen the frontier strategically and assist France's economy by the acquisition of the Saar mines, thus making her industry less dependent on imported coal. Nevertheless, the acquisition of territory in the Rhineland does not seem to have been a major objective for Napoleon himself. If it soon for a while became a prime aim of French policy that was, as will be seen,* rather because of the pressure of French opinion than because of his own conviction that it was desirable or necessary. So, too, if he was now prepared to see a move towards greater unity and the division of the Confederation into three parts, Austria, Northern Germany dominated by Prussia, and a grouping of the Catholic states of the South, this appears to have been less because it was an objective close to his heart than because he believed that a threefold division of Germany would not be prejudicial to France's interests; moreover a regrouping might be a means both of diverting attention for a further time from Rome and of redeeming the pledge he had failed to fulfil in 1859 and securing Venetia at last for Italy.

Venetia, rather than the Rhineland, was thus one of the dominant preoccupations of the Emperor after the apparent settlement of the Roman question by the Convention of September 1864. Not only did he wish to achieve his original aim of freeing Italy 'to the Adriatic', but he was afraid, he said,

* See below, pp. 141–3.

that if he did not do so he would leave his son to sit 'on a barrel of gunpowder'. In May 1866 Lord Cowley reported his own firm impression that Napoleon had determined that the Venetian question '*shall be* settled now', and in the same month Napoleon himself was to tell the Austrian Ambassador that his 'only interest' was to be finished with the Italian question by procuring the cession of Venice.

Meanwhile Bismarck, who long before, at their first meeting in 1855, had reported the Emperor to be 'judicious and amiable, but not so clever as the world thinks him', had been twice to Biarritz to try to gauge Napoleon's intentions. Since 1863 in his dealings with the French Government he had dangled in front of them the bait of territory in the Rhineland as compensation for any major readjustment to Prussia's advantage in Germany. In 1864 he hinted to Napoleon that France might acquire Belgium or Luxemburg, but Napoleon had not responded and had later remarked to Cowley on Bismarck's profuseness 'in giving away what did not belong to him'. In October 1865 the two men had long conversations on the sands or in the Villa Eugénie. It appears from Bismarck's report—Napoleon himself kept no record of what passed—that they discussed a rearrangement of the map which would enable Prussia to create a North German Confederation. There was no question of war, no engagements were entered into. The Emperor neither encouraged Bismarck in his schemes nor asked for compensation for France in the event of a change in the balance of power in Germany. But he betrayed his interest in Venetia and left Bismarck with the impression that he was friendly and in any case unlikely to side with Austria. To some extent Bismarck had succeeded in penetrating Napoleon's mask, whereas it is doubtful indeed whether Napoleon realized the ruthless ability behind the seeming 'madness' of his ebullient visitor's conversation. Thus Bismarck might hope for French neutrality in a German conflict, though he could not be sure of it until the war to come was virtually over.

In view of what happened, it has been suggested that Napoleon at Biarritz blundered badly in not striking a bargain with Bismarck, for, as one historian put it, 'he had a definite article to sell, French neutrality, which the purchaser, Bismarck, needed above all things': by not committing himself he lost a great opportunity to secure from Prussia a specific written agreement to an adjustment of France's eastern frontier towards the Rhine. Though it is hardly any easier for us than it was for Bismarck to discover Napoleon's real designs, the fact that the Emperor did not in 1865 raise the question of compensations supports the view that Venetia and not the Rhineland was still his real concern. Indeed he soon encouraged the growth of Austro-Prussian tension in the hope that Austria in alarm would let Venetia go. When the Austrian Government had refused a suggestion, unscrupulously acquiesced in by Napoleon, that they should yield the province in exchange for Roumania, he gratuitously encouraged the Italians to conclude first a commercial treaty and then a military alliance with Prussia, hoping that the implied threat to Vienna would bring Austria to reason. This alliance of April 1866, moreover, included a clause whereby, in the event of victory, Prussia agreed that Italy should obtain Venetia.

Napoleon's diplomacy, however, was as always fluctuating and tortuous. Having, at first, encouraged the growth of tension between the two German powers, he, in May, perhaps influenced by the disquietude of French opinion at the prospect of a new war in Europe, had resort to his time-honoured expedient of proposing a congress to settle the three questions of Schleswig-Holstein, Italy and the future of the German Confederation, and then, when this was as good as rejected by Austria, sought a direct agreement with her on Venetia. He threatened intervention against her unless in the event of her victory she agreed to cede Venetia to him as the price of his neutrality. The Austrians were taken in by his bluff—he told them mendaciously that Prussia had already promised him the Rhineland—and on June 12 concluded the secret treaty that Napoleon desired. Six days later war was declared.

Neither Napoleon nor most of the experts of the day expected either a short war or a resounding Prussian victory. Napoleon believed that the Austrian army was 'the better of the two—the Prussian the better appointed'; and there is little doubt that he and his advisers expected that the war would be a long-drawn-out struggle which might well end in stalemate, and that then the weary combatants would be only too ready to accept the Emperor as a mediator on his own terms.

How far he had any cut and dried plans for intervening or exploiting a stalemate we do not know, although some historians have pictured him designing to take Belgium or Luxemburg, thereby effacing Waterloo and the humiliating treaties of 1815. But Prussia's crushing victory over the Austrians at Sadowa on July 3, after only three weeks' fighting, was 'a thunder clap in a clear sky', which astonished and stupefied most Frenchmen and caused intense concern in Paris. The Emperor did his best to change the mood to one of rejoicing by giving the maximum publicity to the news which followed at once that Francis Joseph had ceded Venetia to Napoleon and had requested his mediation. But the hard reality of Prussia's dominance of the German situation remained.

On July 5 a first fateful and passionate debate of the Council of Ministers, presided over by the Emperor and attended by the Empress, was held at St. Cloud to determine France's position. On the one hand, Drouyn de Lhuys, supported by the Empress, Persigny, and others, urged that Bismarck should be warned that no territorial changes could be permitted without Napoleon's consent and that France should mobilize and send 50,000 men to the Rhine to support this stand. Then, if Berlin refused to accept the French ultimatum, France could at last make the effective alliance with Austria which Drouyn had been hankering for ever since 1853. On the other hand, Rouher, the powerful Minister of State, Baroche, the Minister of Justice, and La Valette, Minister of the Interior, argued strongly against intervention, invoking the unpreparedness of the French army, the undesirability of alliance with the 'corpse' of Austria, the most resolute foe of nationality, and the probable reactions of public opinion, if Italy, 'forced to justify herself, published documents to show that her treaty with Prussia of 8 April had been, not only approved, but actually promoted by the imperial government'. Despite these arguments, Napoleon, according to the generally received version, at first accepted his Foreign Minister's proposals, and the government's decisions implementing them were to have been published on the following day in the *Moniteur*. But they never appeared because the

Emperor, after a sleepless night, hesitated anew, adjourned the decision on mobilization and eventually, as a result of the discussions which were resumed and continued until the 10th, preferred to rely on diplomacy alone. Again the decisive factors which caused him to change his mind cannot be known for certain: but it is probable that among them were his awareness of France's unreadiness for war, his knowledge that 30,000 men were still tied up in the Mexican enterprise in which he had rashly engaged in 1862,* and his consciousness of the undoubted pacifism of a public now cushioned by material ease and, as Mérimée said, unwilling to risk its skin or 'manger de la vache enragée' for the sake of 'la gloire'. Earlier, in the days of his strength, Napoleon III had often felt powerful enough to ignore opinion: now after the setbacks of the last five years he could much less easily afford to do so, and, increasingly unable to guide it, he more and more became its prisoner. If, however, he now made the crucial error of abdicating a position of strength, French public opinion was his accomplice. As he himself told the Legislative Body in 1867: 'Faced with this conflict, the country resolutely indicated its desire to stay out'.

Meanwhile Bismarck had eased his decision by putting forward terms which were moderate, which corresponded to Napoleon's own ideas, and which Austria was prepared to accept, namely, the dissolution of the 1815 Confederation, the exclusion of Austria from Germany as well as from Italy, the reorganization of Germany north of the Main under Prussian leadership and, soon after, agreement that the South German states should enjoy an 'independent international existence'. A preliminary peace on these lines was concluded at Nikolsburg on July 26 and confirmed at Prague on August 23. Thus, although the Seven Weeks War had been so astonishingly brief and decisive, Napoleon had had the satisfaction of procuring Venetia for Italy, of seeing Austria further humiliated, and of witnessing the further destruction of the settlement of 1815. Moreover, all this, as he reminded the Senate in 1867, had been achieved without the moving of a single French soldier: he had gratified his countrymen by keeping them out of war. But —and here, in French eyes, was once again the great weakness

* See below, pp. 135–6.

of his diplomacy—nothing tangible had been gained for France, whereas Prussia had annexed several territories in North Germany and increased her population by four millions. The balance of power had been drastically altered to France's detriment, Prussia had emerged as a formidable military state, and Napoleon's prestige at home and abroad was gravely damaged, because he had allowed himself to be overtaken by events and had failed to profit by them. As Bismarck himself later pointed out, the intervention of even a small French force at the right moment could have altered the whole military position and enabled Napoleon to secure France's interests by armed mediation.

That opportunity had not been seized. Perhaps it was, as has been suggested, Napoleon's dearest wish 'to appear as the disinterested patron of Italy and Germany'. Perhaps he did genuinely believe that, as he told La Valette in August, the true interest of France was 'not to gain some insignificant increase of territory, but to help Germany establish herself in the most favourable way for her interests and those of Europe'. Perhaps through disinterested patronage of German and Italian unity he might, as a German historian later suggested, have forged a German-French-Italian league, which, more than any other alliance, could have ensured the peace of Europe. But if so, he had few supporters for such views in France, apart from Prince Napoleon and a small number of Republicans, and he had failed to educate the majority of his countrymen to think on such lines. On the contrary, the Legislative Body earlier in the year had loudly applauded Thiers when, in a famous speech on May 3, he had, while urging French non-intervention, denounced the danger of Prussian expansion and a policy which 'would tend to re-establish the ancient German empire by placing the power of Charles V in the north . . . of Germany' and by uniting Prussia in alliance with Italy. Now the majority of Frenchmen felt that Thiers had been right and believed with Marshal Randon that France, too, had been beaten at Sadowa.

Chapter Eight

Colonial Empire and Overseas Adventures

WHEN Louis Napoleon became President of the Second Republic France's overseas possessions were still, with the exception of Algeria, little more than the remnants of the empire which England had destroyed in the Seven Years War and in the long conflict of 1793–1815. They consisted of scattered islands and trading posts or ports of call: in the New World the West Indian sugar islands of Martinique and Guadeloupe; off Newfoundland the fishing stations of St. Pierre and Miquelon, and in South America a neglected stretch of Guiana; in West Africa footholds in Senegal and on the Guinea Coast; on the Indian mainland Pondichéry and four other trading posts; and in the Indian Ocean Bourbon (Réunion) and neighbouring islands. More recently, under the July Monarchy, new trading stations had been set up in Gaboon, the islands of Nosse-Bé and Mayotta off Madagascar had been occupied, and in the Pacific the Marquis Islands had been annexed and a protectorate established over Tahiti. But the total population of these colonial dominions did not exceed 659,000, the great majority of whom were coloured and indigenous.

A momentous new departure had, however, been made by the Restoration Monarchy with the capture of Algiers in 1830, and the decision to retain and consolidate this conquest was to determine the future of a large part of North Africa for decades to come. But the business of pacification had been slow and costly, and was still incomplete. There were many intelligent Frenchmen who, like Louis Philippe himself, had doubted the wisdom of this conquest and regarded it as a liability rather than an asset.

Louis Napoleon, who wrote on so many different topics during his imprisonment at Ham, had not ignored overseas problems. He had discussed at length the failure of the home-grown beet-sugar industry, which had first been established in France in the reign of his uncle; he had considered its relation to colonial production and had urged the abolition of the mercantilist policy of the 'Colonial Pact' whereby all colonial goods had first to be carried to the mother-country. Thus the French colonies would find a new outlet for their sugar and the home-grown sugar would not clash so directly with the colonial product. His interest had also been aroused in a proposed trans-Isthmian canal in Central America. A representative of the states of Guatemala, San Salvador and Honduras had been permitted to visit him in 1844 and had urged him to go to Central America and to put himself at the head 'of this gigantic enterprise'. Louis Napoleon, in prison, was, in his own words, 'all the more disposed to project his mind into imaginary realms and to discuss the possibility of executing plans which he might have had no time to think of had he been leading a more active life'. Negotiations accordingly began, and in 1846 he was informed that the Nicaraguan Government had decided to call this 'grand ouvrage d'art' Canale Napoleone de Nicaragua. In consequence, he had signed a contract whereby, subject to the approval of the Nicaraguan Government, toll and transit rights for fifty years were to be granted to a canal company to be formed by him. Once free in England, he continued to prosecute this design, publishing a brochure setting out the merits of his scheme, trying to enlist the interest of financiers, and even asking Lord Clarendon to obtain a monetary grant from the English parliament. His efforts had, however, been abortive, and the revolution of 1848 in France soon gave him very different preoccupations.

It is noteworthy that the two overseas problems of which he had treated most fully were both largely questions of commerce and economic development. Apart from them, Louis Napoleon's known references to his country's colonies were, like those of many of his countrymen, mostly critical. For example, in 1841, in an article in *Le Progrès du Pas de Calais*, he had derided the July Monarchy's acquisition of Tahiti and the Marquis Islands: France already had too many of these 'imperceptible points on the map'. The more she extended her colonial possessions instead of 'fertilizing' those she already owned, the more French power would be enfeebled. The only two overseas domains which could really become profitable for France, he declared, were Algeria and Guiana. Later, in October 1858, when he had been nearly six years on the throne, he told Lord Cowley that he regretted that France had colonies, since it was so difficult to maintain them in a prosperous state; they were a weakness to the mother country and the necessity of protecting their commerce prevented France from buying in the most advantageous markets.

It might, therefore, be supposed that a ruler who held such views and who had so many cares in Europe would pay little attention to overseas expansion. But the criticisms of the 1840's had been levelled at the government which had put him in prison, while the regrets of 1858 were expressed when he was both moving towards a free-trade policy and speaking to the envoy of the chief colonial power, whose suspicions were easily roused by the expansionist ambitions of other nations, particularly France.

In fact the Second Empire was in many ways a period of initiative, experiment, and adventure in colonial and overseas affairs. Both the Restoration and July Monarchies had retained or added to France's colonies for reasons of prestige and in order to support her position as the chief maritime rival of her old enemy, England. Napoleon III, still more dependent upon prestige and, at the same time, anxious to gratify the army and to conciliate French Catholic opinion, understandably though not invariably gave his blessing to forward policies. But other motives, too, humanitarian and economic, are discernible, so that overseas, as in Europe, it is difficult to say that he had a single aim, an over-all policy specifically aimed at 'colonial development within the framework of French civilization'. It is equally difficult to assess the degree of the Emperor's own direct and continuing concern: but there is much to indicate that this was most considerable in matters relating to economic development and to two of the areas in which he had shown special interest as a young man, namely Algeria and Central America.

Where overseas economic development was concerned the Emperor's liberalism contrasted, as at home, with his political authoritarianism. The constitution of 1852 did away with the colonial representation in parliament instituted by the Second Republic, and the *Sénatus-Consulte* of May 1854 reorganized the relationship of the colonies to the mother country so thoroughly that many of its dispositions were still effective in 1946. It divided the colonies into two groups—the 'great colonies' comprising the Antilles and Réunion, which were regulated by *Sénatus-Consulte*, and the rest, which were in effect governed by Imperial decree for the remainder of the reign. Thus the majority of the French dependencies, apart from Algeria, which presented special problems, were under direct Imperial control. This operated, except for a brief period from 1858 to 1860, through the Ministry of Marine or the Ministry of Marine and Colonies, as it was known from 1860, thus emphasizing the fact that colonies were still thought of largely as props for naval power.

In economic policy, however, Napoleon's liberalism was early in evidence. There was no attempt, despite the discontent of West Indian planters, to reintroduce slavery, which had been abolished in 1848. The tariff on colonial sugars, in which Louis Napoleon had taken such an interest, was lowered as early as 1851, and in the same year he allowed certain Algerian goods free entry into France. After the Anglo-French Commercial Treaty of 1860 it was no longer possible to prevent French colonists from trading with the foreigner and so, in July 1861, a law placed the 'great colonies' on the same footing as the mother country. Thereafter, the measures it prescribed were gradually applied to the remaining colonies. Thus, by 1868, the traditional policy of the Pacte Colonial was at long last abandoned, largely as a result of the Emperor's strong desire for the general expansion of world trade.

In an article in *Le Progrès du Pas de Calais* in 1844 Louis Napoleon had poured scorn on the inability of the July

Monarchy, with an army of 70–80,000 men at its disposal, to pacify Algeria and subdue its 'brigand chieftain', Abd-el-Kader; it was, he said, at peace in Europe and had had fourteen years in which to organize its resources, whereas Napoleon I with only 30,000 men had in fourteen months overthrown the Mamelukes and conquered Egypt. But by 1847 Marshal Bugeaud and his men had succeeded in consolidating France's hold in most of the towns and over the valleys and plateaux inhabited by Arabs, and the number of European settlers had increased to more than 100,000. For over a century there would be no question of any French government relinquishing its grasp of a territory which seemed to contain new reservoirs of wealth and power. For Louis Napoleon, above all, so anxious that his regime should shine in contrast with its predecessors, the abandonment of Algeria was unthinkable. 'The nation', he told Abd-el-Kader, when he released him from captivity in October 1852, 'will never renounce this conquest'. Geographically, its possession enhanced France's position as a Mediterranean power; militarily, it provided a regular training-ground, and many of the generals in the army on whose support the Prince-President ultimately depended were schooled in Algerian warfare; politically it offered a challenge. The problems were to complete the conquest of this 'vast kingdom', as Louis Napoleon called it in 1852, to consolidate the conquest, and to devise for it an effective system of government.

The process of conquest and pacification was continued, slowly under the Second Republic, more rapidly under the Second Empire when financial credits were more readily forthcoming. The tribes of the southern oases and nomads of the desert were gradually subdued and by 1854 French dominion was extended to the edge of the Sahara, while in 1857 Marshal Randon finally overcame the resistance of the Berbers of the mountainous Grande Kabylie between Algiers and Constantine, a proud and numerous people, whom the earlier Turkish overlords had never been able to tame. The conquest was complete, but it was still insecure, liable to the incursions of tribesmen across the ill-defined frontiers with Morocco and Tunisia, and subject to risings and insurrections, which were serious in 1864 and still graver in 1871, a few months after the downfall of the Second Empire.

This insecurity, together with the heterogeneity of the Algerian peoples, the poverty of much of their soil, the influx of European colonists, and the reverence paid to the doctrine of assimilation were the main factors which made the problem of governing Algeria so difficult to solve.

The insecurity strengthened the argument for continuing there the military control which had predominated, except under the Second Republic. But the government's Algerian policies were bedevilled by the constant rivalry between the military and the civilians and much depended on which party gained the Emperor's ear. The influx of European settlers, hungry for land, into the midst of native societies, whose way of life and economy was already dislocated by conquest, had introduced new problems and sources of dissension. The doctrine of assimilation, which assumed that the institutions and society based on the French Revolution were so admirable that the colonies must model themselves on France, was also a stumbling-block, for Parisian bureaucrats too often ignored the complexities of the unfamiliar problems by which they were confronted and believed that they would vanish under a French administrative veneer.

Napoleon III no doubt knew from a book which he had almost certainly read at Ham, the Saint-Simonian Enfantin's *La Colonisation de l'Algérie*, how difficult it would be both to modify native institutions so as to fit them within a European framework and to adapt French institutions so as to fit such a different, African, world. But it is doubtful whether his interest in Algeria before 1848 was more than sporadic, and, when he was in power, his view of the country, like that of many other Frenchmen, appears to have been over-simplified and romantic.

At first the general tendency of his rule was much as might have been expected. Its emphasis was on authoritarianism, assimilation, and material development. The colonists, many of them Republican in sympathy, were deprived of the right to send deputies to parliament in Paris, and the military authorities, with a soldier as Governor-General resident in Algiers, again predominated over the civilians. On the other hand, the assimilationist policy, which had been intensified under the Second Republic, was continued. The system of prefects and departments instituted by the Republic was retained and colonization was encouraged by adherence to the policy of *refoulement* or *cantonnement*, which meant pushing the natives further into the interior in order to increase the area of state land available for the newcomers.

The maintenance of military government could be justified when the conquest of Algeria was still incomplete, but the subjugation of the Grande Kabylie in 1857 brought this long-drawn-out process to an end, and it seemed as though a new and more fruitful era was about to begin. The next seven years are those in which Napoleon's direct personal interest in Algeria was at its most lively. Aware of the great potential importance of the territory, he had already been anxious to mark its special position within the French Empire by having himself crowned King of Algeria as well as Emperor of the French. This project had been discouraged by ministers and constitutional lawyers; but in 1858 he again sought to emphasize the peculiar status of Algeria by appointing his cousin Prince Napoleon to be his Viceroy there. This plan also fell through because of the Prince's reluctance to reside in Algiers. Thereupon the Emperor adopted a Saint-Simonian idea, creating a wholly new Ministry of Algeria and the Colonies, and placing his cousin at its head. This meant the inauguration of a much more liberal civilian regime, but the experiment was short-lived. Friction between the soldiers and the civilians broke out anew, and after only nine months of office the impetuous and none too tactful Prince threw up his post.

Soon afterwards, in the summer of 1860, Napoleon himself spent a month in Algeria and thus became the first French sovereign ever to visit any part of the French dominions overseas. His journey had important consequences. The first was that the soldiers returned to imperial favour, the Ministry for Algeria and the civilian rule that went with it were abolished, and General Pélissier was appointed Governor-General with control over all departments except those of justice, education, and public worship. The second was that the Emperor, moved by what he had seen of the more warlike members of the native populations and by the homage of many splendid chieftains, listened to the French champions of native interests, men like Colonel Lapasset, Baron Jérome David and a Saint-Simonian from Guiana named Ismail Urbain, who urged that the interests of 'three million Arabs' should no longer be sacrificed to those of 100,000 immigrants. As a result, he developed his idea that Algeria was a 'Kingdom' and, to the consternation of the colonists, published in the *Moniteur* of February 6, 1863, a letter to Pélissier, in which he envisaged a division of labour according to the character of the population and declared that Algeria was 'not a colony properly so-called, but an Arab Kingdom. The natives like the colonists have an equal right to my protection and I am Emperor of the Arabs as well as Emperor of the French.'

This remarkable document suggested that the Arabs, too (Napoleon forgot the Berbers and other non-Arab peoples of Algeria), might have a place in the Emperor's vision of a world reorganized on the basis of nationality. But the practical consequences were far from bringing harmony between two sister nations with a single Emperor. The crucial element in the relations between colonist and native was land. The often brutal system of *cantonnement* was now abandoned, and a *Sénatus-Consulte* of April 1863 recognized the collective property of tribes in the lands they had traditionally enjoyed and forbade their purchase by Europeans. But the implementation of the new policy entailed a huge task of surveying and delimitation; until this was complete, colonists could obtain no more land, while the tribes became suspicious and discontented because they were uncertain of their rights. In consequence, individual colonization, no longer backed by the State, virtually came to a halt, while in 1864 there was a fresh outbreak of revolt among many southern tribes.

After this rebellion had been crushed, Napoleon in May 1865 paid a second and longer visit to Algeria. He urged the colonists to treat the Arabs as compatriots, sternly warned the Arabs against fresh insurrections, and told them that perhaps one day their race, 'regenerated and intermingled with the French race (*sic*), would rediscover a powerful individuality'. In a letter to the new Governor-General, Marshal MacMahon, in June of the same year he enunciated a new formula, namely that Algeria was 'at one and the same time an Arab Kingdom, a European colony, and a French camp'.

Unfortunately these exhortations and definitions did not clarify the problem of government and Napoleon's dreams of co-operation and prosperity were not to be realized. Although there is evidence that the native population fared better under military than civil administration, Algeria's history in the last years of the Second Empire was one of disillusionment and disaster. The companies to whom concessions were granted were most of them not the beneficial developers dreamt of by the Saint-Simonians but speculative enterprises which ruinously exploited the lands entrusted to them. The unfortunate peoples were visited by a plague of locusts in 1866, by severe drought in 1867 and by cholera in 1868. The native population of Napoleon's Arab kingdom, consequently, declined. And the Emperor, ailing and preoccupied by set-backs in Europe, could give Algeria little attention or remedy except to yield to the agitation of the colonial interests and in 1870 to endorse the Legislative Body's recommendation for a return to civil government, a change so unpopular with the Arabs that it has been argued that it was the chief, though not the sole, cause of the great insurrection of 1871. Truly Napoleon might say that Algeria was 'a bullet in our leg', and admit, as he did in 1865, that it was a country whose cost was enormous, and a kingdom 'which nobody knew how to govern'. His own equivocal interventions had, if anything, made the task of government still more difficult.

Yet the balance of achievement was not wholly negative. Despite heavy mortality—births did not begin to exceed deaths until the middle 'sixties—the number of colonists since 1848 had more than tripled. The young explorer Duveyrier had carried out a number of remarkable journeys into the Sahara, and, although the rule of a native prince desired by Moslem notables in the early 'thirties had not been permitted, the 'modern civilization' that those notables also looked for had begun to take shape in the form of roads and railways, telegraph lines, dams and other kinds of material construction. Moreover, despite the lack of confidence between conquerors and conquered, which led one disillusioned general to declare that the native peoples were only waiting for a chance to drive the French out of the country, there were Frenchmen like Prévost-Paradol, author of the well-known book *La France Nouvelle* (1868), to whom, given the right policy, Algeria could appear to be France's one hope for the future. For him, it was 'a French land which ought to be peopled, possessed, and cultivated as soon as possible by Frenchmen'. Thereby France might still have a population sufficient to enable her to continue playing a part in world affairs. Before long, he hoped, the Frenchmen of Algeria would spill over into Morocco and Tunis and found a Mediterranean Empire; this would eventually be 'the last resource' of French greatness.

The idea of a French Mediterranean 'empire' or of the Mediterranean being a French 'lake' was not of course a new one. Napoleon I had at one time talked of mastery of the Mediterranean as the chief and constant aim of his policy, and the term 'a French lake' had been used by the important newspaper *Le National* in 1830. More recently Napoleon's nephew had voiced the idea both in 1852 and 1857. But the 'lake' envisaged by Napoleon III was intended to become French through diplomacy and economic power rather than territorial expansion. France herself and Algeria were convenient bases from which Napoleon might hope to bring other Mediterranean lands under a kind of French hegemony. So, too, was Turkey, where, after the Crimean War, French influence was strengthened by the presence of a military mission at Constantinople and by the activities of French engineers and bankers.

On the northern shores of the Mediterranean we have already seen the extent to which Napoleon III was able to control the destinies of Italy. Further east, in the little kingdom of Greece, born in 1830, France exercised influence as one of the protecting powers and that influence increased at the time of the Franco-Austrian war of 1859 which excited Greek hopes of expansion. To the west, he had sought the alliance of Spain at the time of the Crimean War and since then French engineers and financiers had been increasingly active in the Iberian peninsula. Opposite Gibraltar, while disclaiming any designs himself on Morocco, he would have preferred, he told Cowley in 1859, to have a 'civilized neighbour like Spain rather than constant quarrels with the wild hordes which affect the [Algerian] frontier'.

The security of Algeria was indeed an important consideration on the southern shores of the Mediterranean and it dominated France's relations with the Regency of Tunis on Algeria's eastern border. The Regency, like Algiers before 1830, was nominally a Turkish dependency, but its rulers had gradually made themselves independent of Constantinople and, once the French were established in Algeria, had tended to look to France for protection, especially after Turkish re-establishment of control over neighbouring Tripoli in 1835 had seemed to menace their own autonomy. Thus Napoleon's government aimed at preserving the *status quo* in Tunis, while strengthening by diplomacy and economic penetration France's influence there against that of her chief rival, England. Beyond this they had no wish to go, and proposals for annexation, put forward by French consuls in Tunis, were firmly rejected by Paris. Napoleon had no desire to multiply Algerias—one was costly enough—and, when the Regency was faced with bankruptcy in 1867–8, he was ready to share the burden of restoring financial order and to participate in a Debt Commission jointly with England and Italy.

It was further east in Egypt, where French financiers were also active, that Napoleon III scored the most dramatic of his Mediterranean successes. The idea of a canal across the Isthmus of Suez had already been explored by Napoleon I. Towards the middle of the nineteenth century it was given a new impetus by Saint-Simonians such as Enfantin and Chevalier, who saw in it a significant step towards furthering their favourite notion of 'a marriage' between East and West. Their enthusiasm fired that of a talented cousin of the Empress, Ferdinand de Lesseps, who in 1854 founded an international company to promote the construction of a canal and soon afterwards secured a 99 years' concession from the Viceroy of Egypt.

The scheme met with continuous and outspoken opposition from the British Government, and for many years the Sultan of

Turkey, Egypt's suzerain, withheld his consent to it. But Napoleon III perceived its importance both for French interests and for international trade. In 1859, despite England's objections, he gave de Lesseps his open support, and in 1865 it was his intervention which eventually induced the Sultan to issue a *firman* approving the construction of the canal as 'one of the most desirable events in this century of science and progress'. Work began in 1859, Napoleon himself became a shareholder, and ten years later the great labour was completed. The splendid opening ceremony on 17 November, 1869, in which the Empress Eugénie and representatives of most of the ruling houses of Europe took part, was the last but not the least spectacular triumph of the Second Empire and one which ultimately brought great financial benefit to the predominantly French shareholders.

Napoleon III's influence in the Mediterranean from Spain to Greece waned in the 'sixties because France and Spain fell out over Mexico, Italy grew in independence, and the Greeks' affections cooled when he failed to back their 'great idea' of an enlarged Greece which would have meant the disintegration of European Turkey. But at the eastern end of the Mediterranean it was strengthened not only by the building of the Suez Canal in Egypt, but also by French intervention on behalf of Christians in Syria and the Lebanon. In these lands, in which France had long had traditional interests and which were of value to her as a source of raw silk, the ancient rivalry of Catholic Maronites and Moslem Druses had in 1860 flared into hostilities with the resulting massacre of some eleven thousand Christians. As the Turkish Government would not or could not restore order, Napoleon III, head of the power to whom the Sultan by the 'Capitulations' of 1740 had given the right to protect Catholics within the Ottoman Empire, was bound to intervene. Moreover, the massacre gave him a welcome opportunity both to propitiate Catholic opinion at home, recently alienated by his Italian policy, and to put pressure upon the Sultan in the matter of the Suez Canal. Although the European situation and English suspicions obliged him to withdraw his troops within a specified time limit, and although his suggestion for a Syrian buffer state between Turkey and Egypt under Abd-el-Kader as 'Emperor of Arabia' was probably no more than a means of scaring Turkey, his intervention was not fruitless. French diplomacy was subsequently largely instrumental in securing the creation in 1861-4 of an autonomous regime for the Lebanon under a Christian governor which lasted until 1915. This and the fact that French force had been shown in Syria contributed not a little to the revival of French prestige in the Near East. Contemporary observers like the German radical, Julius Fröbel, could see in Napoleon III the regenerator of the Mediterranean world.

The Mediterranean was, however, by no means the only theatre of French overseas enterprise during the Second Empire. Trade and the desire to compete with England led to the expansion of French influence in West and East as well as North Africa. Missionary pressure and the desire to co-operate or compete with England led to intervention in China, to the beginnings of empire in Indo-China, and to the settlement of New Caledonia in the Pacific. Finally, political and, to a much lesser extent, religious calculations as well as long-cherished visions of material wealth induced Napoleon III to interfere in Central America. At one time or another French troops were engaged in every inhabited continent except Australia.

When Louis Napoleon came to power his country's influence in West Africa was confined to a few precarious trading and coaling stations in the Senegal region and on the Guinea coast. But in 1851 the Prince-President approved a more forward policy in Senegal. Military posts were to be established and the French footholds firmly secured. In 1854 the appointment of an able soldier of exceptional administrative vision, General Faidherbe, as governor of Senegal, initiated a period of remarkable advance and consolidation. From his base at St. Louis Faidherbe established a loose but effective protectorate over a wide area, won the confidence of numerous and warring tribes, systematically explored the interior towards the Niger, successfully stimulated the production of ground-nuts and other raw materials (which were exported from the new port of Dakar, created by him in 1857), and tapped the trade of the Sudan. In a space of ten years he laid the foundations of

France's future West African Empire. This, moreover, was a different sort of dominion from that established on the shores of the Mediterranean. Government instructions in 1857 had recognized that 'nothing similar to Algeria could be undertaken in Senegal' and that, therefore, the land should as a general rule be left to the native occupiers. Thus, happier because the climate forbade colonization, the history of Senegal was free from the constant conflict of settler and tribesman.

Similar, though far less striking, advances were also made further south on the Guinea and Ivory coasts through treaties with native chiefs and the establishment of new trading posts in the Gaboon, and in 1869 these various footholds were united, under the command of an admiral, as the 'French Establishments of the Gold Coast and Gaboon', thus providing bases for the notable expansion that would take place under the Third Republic.

The building of the Suez Canal also stimulated French interest in the Red Sea area. In 1862 the territory of Obock opposite Aden was bought from an Abyssinian governor, but this was not to be effectively occupied during the Second Empire. Only in the great island of Madagascar could it be said that the policy favoured by the Ministry of Marine and Colonies was unsuccessful. The complexity of Madagascan politics was not fully understood and this was the one area in the African world where French interests at this time tended conspicuously to lose ground to English for lack of backing and comprehension at home. But Anglo-French rivalry in Africa did not lead to conflict. The two countries were happily still able to settle their differences and to do so without compelling each other to create unwanted protectorates or to annex unwanted territories.

The Suez Canal shortened the route to the Far East but French enterprise there did not wait upon its opening. Napoleon III's policy in Eastern Asia aimed at protecting French Catholic missionaries, who were intermittently persecuted in China and Annam and constantly demanded military and naval support. It also sought to secure for France a strategic base comparable with Britain's Hong Kong or Spain's

Manila. In the 'fifties the main centre of interest was China, where England was the pacemaker for Western demands, while Napoleon firmly adhered to his policy of co-operating with his ally of the Crimean War, despite the constant friction between Englishmen and Frenchmen on the spot and the fact that British and French interests were by no means identical. Thus in 1857–8 French troops eventually joined with British in the capture of Canton, whose Viceroy had refused satisfaction for various grievances, and in 1858 and 1860 they fought alongside British forces in campaigns in North China designed to compel the Chinese Government to honour its undertakings and to open further ports to European trade. In the treaty of 1860, which followed a joint advance upon Peking and the sacking of the Imperial summer palace, Napoleon won satisfaction for Catholic interests but no territorial gain. His designs on the island of Chusan were frustrated by English diplomacy, and for territorial expansion he had had to look further south to Indo-China, where, as early as 1853, a French Foreign Office memorandum had urged the acquisition of a port.

Here, too, in Indo-China French missionaries, often harshly persecuted by the Annamese ruler Tu-Duc, were foremost in urging a forward policy and made a direct approach to Napoleon. Spanish missionaries, too, were among the victims and, late in 1857, Napoleon decided to intervene. He ordered the French admiral in command of the fleet operating in Chinese waters to combine with Spanish forces from Manila, seize the port of Tourane, and, if possible, establish a French protectorate over Cochin-China. The enterprise proved more difficult than was expected. The rising against Tu-Duc confidently predicted by the missionaries did not take place, the European troops were ravaged by disease, and, despite their occupation of Saigon, Tu-Duc refused to treat, so that considerable reinforcements had to be sent. It was not until 1861 that the Annamese Emperor capitulated and agreed to cede to France the three eastern provinces of Cochin-China, permit the free exercise of Catholic worship in his dominions, and accept a kind of protectorate. To the Chambers, Napoleon in 1863 held out a noble prospect of 'exploiting the immense resources of these countries and of civilizing them by means of commerce'. But in fact, increasingly involved in Mexico, he appears to have hesitated over the retention of new territorial commitments in South-East Asia. It was only the firmness of Chasseloup-Laubat, the able Minister of Marine and Colonies, which caused him in 1865 to go back on his decision to retrocede the provinces in exchange for commercial advantages. The result was a steady French penetration of this part of South-East Asia. Already in 1863 Doudart de Lagrée, a remarkable French explorer, had secured a treaty whereby the decadent Siamese vassal state of Cambodia accepted a French protectorate, and in 1866–7 the remainder of Cochin-China was wrested from Annam. Thus by 1870 the foundations of a new French dominion were laid in the valley of the Mekong, a territory which was long to be governed by admirals, just as Algeria was governed by generals, and whose future would be hardly less controversial than that of France's colony opposite Marseilles.

Such pattern as is discernible in these more or less distant enterprises largely conforms with that of the Second Empire in Europe. Until the middle 'fifties the emphasis is on the consolidation, material development, or territorial rounding-off of France's existing overseas possessions: so in Europe these were the years when Louis Napoleon, as President and then as Emperor, was feeling his way and then securing his position through participation in the Crimean War, a major commitment which permitted little diversion elsewhere. The middle years of his reign, when his prestige was at its height, are also those when his overseas policies were most varied and venturesome. The distant expeditions, he himself said, were not 'the execution of a premeditated plan'; they arose from 'the force of circumstances'—a phrase he often used. But these expeditions and enterprises jostled hard upon one another, the annexation of New Caledonia (1854), and Faidherbe's driving forward in Senegal (1853–6), the conquest of the Berber strongholds (1857) and the new experiments in governing Algeria (1858–65), economic penetration in the Mediterranean area generally, the beginning of the Suez Canal (1859), the China Wars (1858 and 1860), the first annexationist moves in Indo-

China (1862), and the Syrian expedition (1860–1). The activity, if not always fruitful, is impressive in its extent and variety. Then, in the last seven years of the reign, as the Emperor's grip on affairs is enfeebled and troubles crowd upon him at home, the picture changes again; the overseas momentum slows down nearly everywhere except in Indo-China, and in Mexico and Algeria there is disaster and embarrassment. Yet, so late as February 1865, he could still paint a grandiose picture of the temple of war closing, as one overseas force after another came home: 'With pride we shall be able to inscribe on a new triumphal arch these words: "To the glory of the French armies, for the victories won in Europe, Asia, Africa and America"'.

The Mexican expedition was once called by Rouher 'the great idea of the reign' (*la grande pensée du règne*) and subsequently this phrase was used in derision by Napoleon's adversaries. Yet in many ways the conceptions underlying the expedition were imaginative and showed once again that Napoleon was a ruler who had an acute perception of the new forces at work in his time. In the New World, which both he and some of his Saint-Simonian advisers such as Michel Chevalier had visited, he believed that there were still vast reservoirs of wealth to be tapped and he was impressed by the great and growing might of the United States. But he had little more love for this Protestant power in North America than has his successor as master of France a hundred years later, General de Gaulle; and he believed that if the Latin countries were to count in the years to come they, too, must take part in industrial advance and build economic empires. Here in the New World there seemed unexpectedly to open an opportunity for France to acquire a rich sphere of economic influence and to construct a barrier in the way of the southward advance of what, in an undated memorandum of the 'forties, Louis Napoleon had called 'this colossal power', the United States. This opportunity he seized with both hands, but it proved to be far less golden than he expected and his intelligence services were, not for the first time, faulty.

Napoleon's interest in Central America was, of course, no

new development. It goes back at least to his concern with the
proposed Nicaraguan Canal when he was a prisoner at Ham.
Moreover, it has recently been shown that the canal which he
had been invited to sponsor was part of a wider scheme whereby he might become President, not of Ecuador, as Lord
Malmesbury erroneously recorded, but of a united Central
American state, for which its promoters hoped to secure British
protection. In a brochure of the late 'forties, written to forward
the canal scheme, he had alluded to the desirability of seeing
'Central America become a flourishing and considerable State,
which will restore the balance of power by erecting in Spanish
America a new centre of industrial activity powerful enough
to give birth to a strong feeling of nationality and, by supporting Mexico, to prevent further encroachments from the
north'. Here already in germ were three main elements in 'the
great idea': 'industrial activity' or economic development,
'nationality', and the 'balance of power'; in other words, he
wished to see the building in Central America of a strong and
prosperous nation capable of halting the southward advance of
the United States, which had but recently annexed large areas
of Mexico. But in 1849 Prince Louis Napoleon envisaged these
developments as taking place under English auspices, whereas
in 1861 the Emperor Napoleon saw them as a splendid means
of enhancing French power and prestige.

In 1848 he had to explain to his Central American friends
that he was far too preoccupied with affairs in France to trouble
further with canals in Nicaragua. But his interest in that part
of the world was only dormant, and by 1854 it appears that,
perhaps under the influence of Chevalier, he had come to the
conclusion that the key to the future of Central America lay
not in Nicaragua but in Mexico with its known but un-
developed mineral wealth. Mexico, which had won independence from Spain in 1821, was, like many other Latin American
Republics, torn by racial and religious dissensions. These involved it in intermittent civil war, which led in 1857 to the
triumph of the strongly anti-clerical 'Liberals', headed by a
man of Indian origin named Juarez, and to the imposition of a
secularizing constitution much to the discomfiture of the Creole
aristocracy and its clerical supporters. Now, from Napoleon's

point of view, order and stable government were essential pre-
requisites of economic development, and he did not welcome
the success of Juarez who in return for American support was
ready to grant considerable economic concessions to the United
States. Already in 1857 Napoleon had told Disraeli of his 'wish
and willingness to assist in establishing a European dynasty in
Mexico'. In 1858 he was ready to listen to one of the Mexican
exiles, Hidalgo, who had gained access to him through the
Empress, ever a champion of Catholic interests, and who represented that there was a strong party ready to re-establish a
monarchy there if only a suitable sovereign and sufficient help
were forthcoming from some European power.

Undoubtedly Napoleon's interest was aroused; but if he
listened, he did not commit himself. For one thing, the Italian
war was soon to be his main preoccupation; for another, the
United States had made it plain that they would regard European interference in Mexico as a breach of the Monroe
Doctrine.

But by the autumn of 1861 the situation had greatly altered.
Italy had been unified apart from Rome and Venetia; the
United States were paralysed by the Civil War which had
broken out between North and South in April 1861; and in
July Juarez, who had taken over a nearly empty treasury, had
suspended payment on all debts to foreign bondholders.
Juarez's action and the temporary impotence of the United
States gave Napoleon his opportunity. The interests of British
and Spanish as well as French nationals were damaged by
Juarez's refusal to pay his creditors, so that in the autumn the
Emperor was able to negotiate a convention whereby the three
powers agreed to send a military expedition to put pressure
upon Juarez to meet his obligations. At the same time he
secretly endorsed the idea of a monarchical restoration and,
realizing that a French prince would arouse too much jealousy,
countenanced an approach to a younger brother of the Emperor
Francis Joseph of Austria, the Archduke Maximilian.

Thus the Mexican adventure began under seemingly favourable auspices. There is little doubt that Napoleon at this stage
believed that the show of force by the three powers would be
enough to provoke a rising against Juarez, whose government

would collapse, and that the Mexican royalists and French diplomacy would then do the rest, re-establishing a monarchy under Maximilian who would grant the desired economic privileges to France.

Unfortunately, the three powers from the first disagreed about the claims they were to present to Juarez and about their ultimate objectives. Moreover, the landing of some 9,000 troops (two-thirds of them Spaniards) on the Vera Cruz coast did not precipitate the looked-for rising. Napoleon, who on the eve of the Italian war had told Cavour to mind his finances and supplies: 'One cannot be too careful in one's preparations' —had shown singular credulity in believing the Mexican exiles' stories and extraordinary negligence in not preparing himself with the maximum of accurate information before attempting to implement his 'great idea'. The Mexicans were no more ready to rise at the call of the European in 1862 than the Annamese had been in 1858.

The consequence was that the Spaniards, who wanted not a Hapsburg but a Bourbon prince, and the English, who had no interest in overturning the Mexican government, having obtained some pecuniary satisfaction, soon withdrew. The French forces were left in isolation in 'that land of yellow fever and black vomit', as Disraeli called it, where for the time being, as in Annam, they suffered far more from the climate than from the foe.

Thus the first phase of the adventure was over. The French Foreign Office had never been eager for embroilment in Mexico and now it might well seem that France, too, could withdraw after securing financial compensation. What followed, however, showed that for Napoleon the financial issue was simply a pretext for securing a foothold in Mexico. He was determined to go ahead with his plans, and, since the show of moderate force had failed, he was prepared, despite warnings from the Spanish general Prim about the difficulties of the enterprise, to use much greater force to achieve his real ends. In July 1862 he personally instructed the French commander, General Forey, to take Mexico City, summon a constituent assembly, advise it to restore the throne and invite Maximilian to become Emperor. Of Catholic interests and France's financial claims Napoleon made no mention.

The French troops were increased from some 2,500 to 20,000 (later to 30,000) and the offensive began in February 1863; but once again the looked-for popular support was not forthcoming. The French forces were checked in front of Puebla in May, as they had been checked before Rome in 1849, and, since this check, too, appeared to be an insult to national honour which had to be avenged, Napoleon was all the more dogged in the pursuit of his 'great idea'. Moreover, the eventual fall of Mexico City did not mean the collapse of resistance. Nationality in Mexico, as in Spain in 1808, worked against and not for a Napoleon, and Juarez could still harry the French from north and south.

Under such circumstances it was impossible to summon a freely elected parliament to vote for a monarchical regime. The French commander had to resort to a hand-picked Assembly of Notables who duly offered the crown to Maximilian. But when Maximilian, who had accepted Napoleon's earlier overtures with alacrity, at last arrived in Mexico in 1864, he proved to be too weak a personality to dominate an extraordinarily difficult situation. The government he set up was therefore unable to attract any large measure of Mexican support and depended for its maintenance on the French army.

Thus Napoleon's land of promise turned out to be a Serbonian bog. He had had to keep troops in Rome for fifteen years to bolster up the Pope and now it looked as though he might have to maintain a far larger body of men indefinitely in Mexico to prop up Maximilian. Indeed, before leaving Europe Maximilian had exacted a promise that Napoleon would lend him the support of French troops for a certain time, and in January 1864 he had been assured that the troops would leave Mexico only by stages and when they could do so without compromising the existence of the new government.

Unfortunately for both Emperors (for Maximilian took the title of Emperor of Mexico), these pledges were untenable. Napoleon's position in Mexico was far less defensible than his position in Rome. In Rome it was clear that he was defending French Catholic interests; in Mexico he had no aim that could be publicly avowed as in the French national interest. French public opinion, critical of the expedition from the first, became increasingly reluctant to grant credits for expenditure which brought no visible return. Yet, obstinate and obsessed by his Mexican dream as he was, Napoleon might still have braved opposition at home but for the ending of the American Civil War in 1865 and the deterioration of the European situation in 1866. In 1862 his decision to carry on with the implementation of the 'great idea' was not such folly as it might seem in retrospect; for he could still reckon that the Southern States, whose independence, France like England had refused to recognize, might win the American Civil War and that North America would be permanently divided. But in 1865 the victorious Northern States, who had regarded Napoleon's neutrality during the Civil War as unfriendly, were in no mood to tolerate continued French interference in a neighbouring state. They resumed their aid to Juarez and launched a masterly diplomatic campaign against the European intruder. The threat was clear. Napoleon, who could not face war with the United States as well as war with Juarez and revolt in Algeria, was obliged to tell Maximilian that he would have to withdraw his troops by stages, even though the Mexican monarchy was not securely established. The appeals of Maximilian's wife, the Empress Charlotte, who personally crossed the Atlantic to see Napoleon and Eugénie in the summer of 1866, were in vain. By then the Austro-Prussian war had broken out and it was more than ever impracticable for Napoleon to keep 30,000 men locked up in Mexico.

The last French troops left the country of disillusionment in December 1866 and after that the miserable end was not long in following. Already the Empress Charlotte, frantic at Napoleon's treachery and her own failure to win European aid, had gone mad. Six months after the departure of the French soldiers in May 1867, Maximilian, who had changed his mind about abdicating, was taken prisoner by Juarez's men and shot. The House of Hapsburg, which suffered so many tragedies between 1848 and 1918, had made its sacrifice to Napoleon's 'great idea'. The occasion was to be immortalized by the Impressionist painter Manet in a picture of which his fellow

Impressionist, Renoir, said that 'the beauty of the black tones makes up for the brutality of the subject'.

The Mexican adventure, so particularly Napoleon III's own idea and commitment throughout all its stages, vividly illustrates the qualities and still more the defects which had already shown themselves in his conduct of policy in Europe—imaginativeness and obstinacy, opportunism and equivocation, wilfulness and negligence. Of all his overseas enterprises it was the most disastrous. It dealt an irreparable blow to his prestige and cast a deep shadow over the remaining years of the Second Empire.

Chapter Nine

The 'Black Clouds' and the Liberal Empire, 1866–70

THE last four years of the Second Empire have about them an air of classic tragedy and impending doom. They are overshadowed by the 'defeat' of Sadowa, the Mexican fiasco, the Roman complication, and the Prussian danger. They see the French nation dominated by the fear of war but loath to make the sacrifices necessary to avert it. They see its ruler sick and ageing, his grip enfeebled, his freedom of action increasingly restricted. They are clouded by economic recession and embittered by growing industrial unrest and by the violent attacks of a truculent opposition and an unbridled press. Yet the gloom is not unrelieved: the exhibition of 1867 was an eloquent witness to France's material progress; the opening of the Suez Canal in 1869 was a triumph of French achievement; and in 1870 a new constitution and a plebiscite appeared to promise the Empire a fresh lease of life and renewed stability.

Napoleon III's aims during this last period were laudable enough from the point of view of French interests. They were to restore France's prestige through some new accession of territory, to strengthen her international position by reforming her army and winning allies, to emphasize anew her devotion to peaceful conquests by giving a fresh impetus to the economy, and, eventually, to 'crown the edifice' by the concession of further political liberty. But, doubtful of his country's real strength, lacking not in intelligence but in will power, wedded to his old conspiratorial methods, no longer daring to ignore opinion, he lacked the driving force to prosecute many of these aims with success. In consequence, he was outwitted by superior antagonists, imprisoned by the past contradictions of his policy abroad, and frustrated by the growing power of his critics at home.

Nowhere were his efforts more lamentable than in the field of foreign policy, which was so peculiarly his own domain. In September 1866 a circular to the diplomatic corps, published in the *Moniteur*, sought to justify the changes consequent upon Sadowa in language which, if strangely far-sighted, was more lofty than convincing to contemporary Frenchmen. The coalition of the Northern Courts, this so-called La Valette circular pointed out, had now gone the way of the treaties of 1815, and in the new era 'an irresistible power' was impelling the peoples to unite themselves in great masses by causing the lesser states to disappear. An enlarged Prussia and a free Italy were now part of a new Europe of stronger and more homogeneous states. This Europe would be the better able to withstand those giants, Russia and the United States of America, each of which might 'before another century has expired, contain a hundred million inhabitants'. 'The Emperor does not believe that the greatness of a country depends on the weakness of its neighbours; he sees a true balance only in the satisfied wishes of Europe.'

Unfortunately France herself was far from satisfied and Napoleon knew it. Even before the outbreak of the Austro-Prussian war in June 1866 he had been made aware of the criticism to which he might be subjected if the balance of power in Central Europe was radically altered without any gain for France. Hence there began the frenzied and undignified quest for territorial compensation in the Rhineland, Luxemburg and Belgium, which was an obsession with French statesmen and diplomats, until in May 1867 it appeared to be hopeless to pursue it further.

This quest began in May and June 1866, when Napoleon indicated to Prussia that he could support her in her approaching war against Austria only if France were recompensed—'the eyes of my country are fixed on the Rhine'—and then pointed out that, since the German Confederation had been established in 1815 by international agreement, its status could not be altered without the consent of France who would require a *quid pro quo*. Bismarck replied, as he was to reply again more

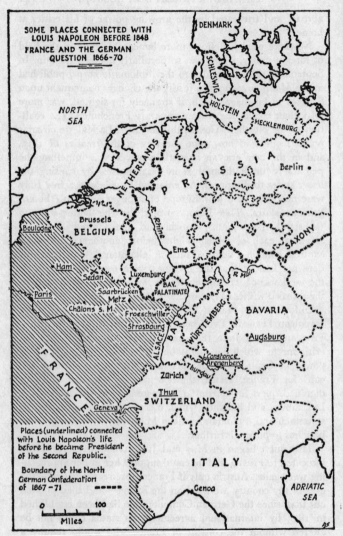

SOME PLACES CONNECTED WITH
LOUIS NAPOLEON BEFORE 1848
FRANCE AND THE GERMAN
QUESTION 1866–70

NORTH
SEA

DENMARK
SCHLESWIG
HOLSTEIN
MECKLENBURG

NETHERLANDS
PRUSSIA
Berlin

Boulogne
Brussels
BELGIUM
Luxemburg
SAXONY
R. Rhine
Ems
R. Main

Ham
Sedan
Saarbrücken
BAV.
PALATINATE
Paris
Metz
Châlons s. M.
Froeschwiller
Strasbourg
ALSACE
BADEN
WÜRTTEMBERG
BAVARIA
Augsburg

Constance
Arenenberg
Zürich
Thurgau
Thun
SWITZERLAND
Geneva

F R A N C E

ITALY

Genoa

ADRIATIC
SEA

Places (underlined) connected
with Louis Napoleon's life
before he became President
of the Second Republic.

Boundary of the North
German Confederation
of 1867–71   -----

0   100
Miles

France and the German Question 1866–70

forcefully later in the year, that he could not surrender German territory, and at the same time suggested, as he had suggested before, that he would see no objection to French expansion in French-speaking lands—in other words he once again sought to divert Napoleon from Germany by proffering the bait of Belgium which was not his to bestow.*

His answers should have been a warning of the probable difficulties of obtaining compensation in the Rhineland unless France backed her demands with a show of force. Yet three weeks after Sadowa, Napoleon, who had made the fatal decision to renounce armed mediation, was under renewed pressure to save France's face by some territorial acquisition and returned to the charge. On July 23 Drouyn de Lhuys, his Foreign Minister, instructed Benedetti, the French Ambassador in Berlin, to ask for the restoration of France's 1814 frontiers with the addition of Luxemburg, as compensation for Prussia's annexations in North Germany, since these had not been included in the terms for a peace settlement put forward by Napoleon. This was a demand that Bismarck was scathingly to refer to as 'the hotel-keeper's bill', a bill which he was determined not to pay. For the moment, since peace with Austria was not yet assured, he temporized, alleging the difficulty of persuading the Prussian King to agree to such an arrangement. But, when on August 5 Benedetti returned with more specific proposals, the preliminaries of peace had been signed and Prussia's position was therefore much stronger. Bismarck bluntly replied that he would not yield 'a single German village' and that if France persisted in her demands he would march against her with 800,000 men. At the same time, to Napoleon's embarrassment, he informed a French newspaper correspondent that the French Emperor had made demands which were unacceptable. The unhappy Napoleon, now weary and ill at Vichy, did not stay to consider whether Prussia was in any condition to carry out her minister's threat. He weakly disavowed Drouyn de Lhuys, who was thereupon obliged to resign.

But the Minister of State, Rouher, to whom Napoleon entrusted the conduct of foreign affairs for an interim period,

* See above, p. 112.

was another of those who were convinced of the need to mollify French opinion by territorial gain, and so he, too, pursued the quest for compensation. Since Bismarck had more than once hinted that he would not oppose French expansion elsewhere on France's eastern frontier, Benedetti was now instructed to offer Prussia an offensive and defensive alliance in return for the open cession to France of the Grand Duchy of Luxemburg and for a secret agreement whereby Prussia would agree to France's annexation of Belgium when the opportunity arose.

The offer was naïve, for a French alliance, which might have been attractive to Bismarck in 1865, was now of no interest when Prussia had roundly defeated Austria, was on good terms with Russia, and had no fear of England. But Bismarck did not reject it out of hand: he raised his price and then allowed negotiations to drag out in such a way as to give him the opportunity to lead Napoleon into still further embarrassment. He raised his price by indicating that the French offer might interest him, but only if France now consented to the completion of German unification. This in effect meant the renunciation of the principle of a tripartite Germany, which the French Government had lately been claiming as one of the merits of the new dispensation in Central Europe and as one whose maintenance was essential to their interests. But, just as Napoleon in 1859-60 had renounced his plan for an Italy in four parts in order to secure Nice and Savoy, so now he was ready to perform a new *volte-face* and abandon the division of Germany into three parts in order to secure Luxemburg and perhaps Belgium. Accordingly, on August 29 Benedetti submitted to Bismarck a draft treaty embodying the French proposals and including a clause in which France undertook not to oppose a federal union between the States of South Germany and the North German Confederation. Bismarck thereupon pocketed the draft for future use—he published it in the London *Times* after war had broken out in 1870 as evidence of the aggressive character of French policy—and allowed the negotiations to go to ground. They now had still less object for him, since he had meanwhile adroitly used Napoleon's earlier demands for German territory to persuade the governments of the Southern states that France was a

menace to their independence and to induce them to conclude
secret offensive and defensive alliances with Prussia.

The acquisition of Luxemburg and Belgium was a far more
difficult problem than that of Nice and Savoy. Nice and Savoy
had been Cavour's to dispose of and he had had further need
of Napoleon's good will. The position of Luxemburg and
Belgium was very different and the status of Luxemburg almost
as complicated as that of the duchies of Schleswig and
Holstein whose fate had precipitated the German question.
The sovereign of this strategically important, partly German,
partly French-speaking Grand Duchy, was the King of the
Netherlands, but the duchy itself had been a part of the
German Confederation of 1815 and so, as a federal fortress,
the city of Luxemburg had been garrisoned by Prussian troops.
These troops were still in occupation, although, as a result of
the Austro-Prussian war and the remoulding of Germany, the
old Confederation had been dissolved.

Since Bismarck's dilatory tactics eventually made it clear
that Prussia was uninterested in the proffered French alliance,
Napoleon early in 1867 informed him that he proposed to
negotiate the purchase of the Grand Duchy directly with the
Dutch King (when later this news came out in Paris it was
said that the Emperor was like the hunter who returning with
an empty bag (i.e. without the Rhineland) buys a hare (Luxemburg) in the market). He was given to understand that Bismarck
had no objection and an agreement was on the point of being
signed, when Bismarck in Machiavellian fashion intervened to
frustrate Napoleon's plans. He arranged for a question to be
asked in the North German parliament about the future of
Luxemburg, declared this was of international significance,
and added that he hoped to be able to protect German interests
by peaceful negotiation. German nationalist opinion was at
once unleashed and the King-Grand Duke drew back in
alarm, especially after Bismarck, never sparing of threats, early
in April menaced him with war. Napoleon was naturally ex-
tremely angry, and the now widespread anti-Prussian feeling
in France grew still more when Bismarck chose this time,
perhaps in order to discourage French belligerence, to reveal
the existence of his secret alliances with the South German

states. If this was his object, the stratagem was successful. The warlike tones in Paris died away and France and Prussia both consented to submit the Luxemburg question to a conference of the Powers in London. The upshot was that Luxemburg was put out of Napoleon's reach by being made a second Belgium, its independence maintained and its 'perpetual' neutrality guaranteed. His only satisfaction, one much too slight to restore his prestige in the way he had hoped, was that the Prussian garrison was to be withdrawn and the fortress of Luxemburg to be dismantled. The Emperor and his people were perhaps relieved that peace had been preserved, but neither could be proud of the outcome. The Luxemburg affair strengthened the widespread conviction that war with Prussia was sooner or later inevitable. In August, in a speech at Lille, Napoleon himself admitted that black clouds were darkening the horizon and that France had met with reverses.

As for the independent kingdom of Belgium, whose neutrality had been guaranteed by the Powers in 1839, this was clearly still more difficult for Napoleon to acquire, even though its incorporation with France would have been in accordance with the thesis of La Valette's circular that the big nationalities were destined to absorb the smaller states.

Here again, it is not easy to know whether it was an objective to which Napoleon himself attached vital importance, although its acquisition was a topic on which he touched from time to time: in 1855, for instance, he had told Prince Albert that it and the left bank of the Rhine were necessary to him for the security of his dynasty, in 1862 he had jokingly said to a Belgian lady that her country would one day 'fall like a ripe pear' into France's mouth, and in 1865 it had been mentioned in the interview at Biarritz with Bismarck. But Belgium was fruit forbidden by England—in 1852 the British government had reacted sharply when the Prince-President had adopted a threatening attitude towards Belgium because of a tariff war and violent criticism of him in the Belgian press, and in 1855 Prince Albert had retorted that, if France attempted to take Belgium and the Rhineland, there would be 'a great war'. Now, after the failure of the quest for compensations and in view of

France's strained relations with Prussia, it would seem that Napoleon could hardly risk antagonizing England anew.

Yet in 1868–9 an issue arose which caused considerable coolness and aroused English suspicions that, in Lord Clarendon's words, the Emperor was making 'a sneaking attempt to incorporate Belgium by means of a railway company and its employés'. This was in effect an attempt on the part of the powerful French Compagnie de l'Est, supported by the French Government, to take over two Belgian railways, an attempt which could have strategic and political implications and which was foiled by the opposition of Belgian coal-owners and by the Belgian parliament's hasty passage of a law against railway concessions to foreigners. Once again Napoleon, angered by this new check and, wrongly believing with other Frenchmen that 'Belgium would not be behaving so arrogantly if Prussia were not behind her', spoke of possible war. But it was England, not Prussia, who backed Belgian resistance to this French encroachment, and, in the end, heeding England's warnings, the Emperor agreed that the dispute should be referred to a mixed commission. In such circumstances the Austrian Chancellor's suggestion that Belgium and France should enter into a customs union had no hope of success. Belgium, like Luxemburg, was to retain her independence inviolate for forty years after Napoleon himself had passed away. But the realistic Bismarck, for once not implicated, was recorded as having remarked in 1870 that Napoleon should have occupied Belgium and held it as a pledge—'he is, and remains, a muddle-headed fellow'. Bismarck would have agreed with the words that Napoleon himself had written long before with regard to Switzerland: 'For a small state the phantom of neutrality is merely a chimera . . . Men put their trust in a treaty signed by all the Powers; but the different states are never held back by chill respect for treaties; it is the irresistible force of the moment which causes them to act together or divides them.'

The frustration of this move for economic penetration abroad was the more unwelcome because of economic setbacks at home and the growing criticism of the unorthodox financial methods which had earlier been so successful.

The decade 1860–70 has been called that of France's 'real' industrial revolution. It had been inaugurated by the commercial treaty with England * and by Napoleon's celebrated letter to Fould, published in the *Moniteur* of January 15, 1860, a letter which echoed the famous Bordeaux speech of 1852 proclaiming that the Empire meant peace. Now, the Italian war over, Napoleon had returned to this theme, declared the need for 'the development of the national wealth', and invited Frenchmen to inaugurate with him 'a new era of peace . . . and to ensure that France may reap its benefits'. In particular, he had emphasized the importance of completing the great work of improving France's communications by road, rail and water, and of reducing freight charges in order to enable French goods to compete with the products of foreign industry. Thus a new impetus was given to a vast programme of public works with all the expenditure that this entailed. The 'sixties witnessed a further extension of the railway lines, so that by 1870 there were 23,500 kilometres of track whereas there had been only 3,600 in 1852. Production in some of the metallurgical industries in particular rose phenomenally, and in industry generally there was discernible a growing specialization, greater financial and technical concentration, and increasing mechanization. Foreign trade continued to expand, although the volume of exports began to slow down. The national income went on rising at the rate of approximately 1 per cent per annum. Moreover, although it is difficult to speak of any general improvement in the standard of living of the poorer classes, there is evidence that real wages rose, at any rate in certain large industries and urban centres.

Thus, the overall picture could appear to be one of continuing and remarkable prosperity. In August 1862 *The Economist*, while questioning how far this was due to Napoleon and his 'system', had written in glowing terms of France's achievements since 1852 and the general air of well-being: 'wherever the traveller strays, he sees the reign of growth and prosperity; whatever town he enters, he sees new symptoms of progress and of hope; whatever new district he visits, he finds some

* See above, pp. 61–2.

trace of the same pervading and omnipresent spirit. In the capital the change is not only considerable, but wonderful'.

Yet difficulties had already begun and were to increase. France might continue at peace in Europe, but uncertainty of the Emperor's intentions made men doubt its permanence, and garrisoning Rome and Algeria and sending expeditions to China, Syria and Mexico were ventures for which Frenchmen could see little return. Moreover, in the first half of the decade French commerce had suffered as a result of events in the United States, and a financial scandal, the Mirès affair of 1860-2, had shaken the French business world. The American Civil War for a while deprived French cotton manufacturers of the supplies of American raw cotton, of which they had been importing increasing quantities since 1845, and caused much hardship in the industry between 1861 and 1865. The American Morrill Tariff Act, a highly protectionist measure introduced by Lincoln's government in 1861, damaged the French export trade to the United States so gravely that it did not recover during the nineteenth century, the silk industry of Lyons, the ribbon makers of St. Étienne and the embroiderers of Lorraine being particularly severely hit. As for the financial scandal, one of its most significant consequences had been that it had encouraged two of the most influential men about the Emperor, the former Orleanists Morny and Fould, to set their face against the unorthodox methods of finance hitherto so characteristic of the regime and to join such conservative financiers as Rothschild and Talabot in campaigning for stricter public control of expenditure and for an unadventurous policy without fresh loans or taxes.

The sumptuous reception of Napoleon III by Baron James de Rothschild at his château at Ferrières in December 1862 had symbolized the growing return to influence of former notables of the Orleanist world of politics and finance. The financier and his associates represented forces so powerful that the Emperor could not ignore them, but they were forces basically hostile to the benevolent and open-handed 'imperial democracy' for which Napoleon stood, and, consciously or not, they played a considerable part in hampering his schemes both for the extension of French economic influence abroad and for stimulating a new boom at home. A curious example of this was provided by the history of the Latin Monetary Union.

In 1862 the new Kingdom of Italy had paid Napoleon the compliment of modelling its monetary system upon the proposals of the most recent commission of inquiry in France. But when the monetary difficulties of some of France's neighbours led them in 1865 to turn to her for guidance she failed to make the most of her opportunity. It is highly probable that Napoleon himself, who had once described uniform currencies as one of his uncle's objectives, now hoped to give the European nations a lead in monetary policy, just as earlier he had in tariff reform. But at the conference in 1865 which established the Latin Monetary Union between France, Italy, Belgium and Switzerland, despite the general desire of the delegates for a gold standard, the influence of the Bank of France and the narrow interests of French conservative financiers prevailed to maintain the *status quo* and a bimetallic policy. This was undoubtedly one of the reasons which prevented the new Union from becoming the nucleus of a much wider organization and from making any further recruits except for one in 1868, namely Greece, a small state described by the Union's historian as then 'economically unsound, convulsed by political struggles, and financially rotten'.

In the spring of 1867, when the Luxemburg affair was over, the Emperor spoke again of his desire to launch a loan to finance public works and also of his wish to reduce certain taxes. 1867 was the year of the second great Paris Exhibition which might, it was hoped, give a new stimulus to the economy, for all agreed that it far outshone the exhibition of twelve years earlier. It had more than double the number of participants. It displayed the materials and weapons of the industrial age to come and looked forward to the twentieth century. It bore witness to France's own great technical progress. It attracted kings and princes from all over Europe and from as far away as Japan, and Napoleon had an imperial summer receiving them with his usual graciousness and presiding over perhaps the most brilliant of all the many brilliant Parisian 'seasons' of his reign. But it was the last such triumph and it would be long before monarchs of the Great Powers would again think Paris worth an official visit.

In fact, there were already black clouds on the economic and social as well as on the political horizon. Despite the exhibition, a new recession set in, and, although this recession of 1867-8, like its predecessor in 1861-3, was mild compared with the depressions of the Restoration and July Monarchy, it deeply perturbed the affluent society of the Second Empire. The protectionists, who had never disarmed, once again blamed the Emperor's free-trade policy for their economic ills. The orthodox financiers and their friends in parliament regarded government expenditure with a still more critical eye; while the now constant fear of war contributed to loss of confidence in business circles and to a period of economic stagnation. This lack of confidence and feeling of insecurity was increased by the multiplication of workers' organizations and of strikes, which was especially marked in 1869 and 1870. When there was also a new 'affaire', involving the collapse of the great financial empire of the Péreires themselves, it was no wonder that the Emperor was unable to wave a Saint-Simonian magician's wand and obtain the freedom and money he wanted to initiate a further period of prosperity. The money was there, but it was not forthcoming—'the milliard', it was said, 'went on strike' and the equivalent of a twentieth of the national income, which might have been profitably invested, remained idle in the Bank of France.

Some of the older banks had begun to experiment with new methods and there is no hard and fast differentiation between the old and new; yet a conspicuous theme in the financial history of the Second Empire was the bitter feud between the Rothschilds and other older establishments, including the Bank of France, on the one hand, and the upstart Péreires on the other, whose success, unorthodox methods and vast pretensions had aroused furious jealousies and personal antagonisms. These two great interests came into collision in Austria, in Italy, and in many parts of France itself. An investment bank normally requires a rapid turnover of capital, but the Péreires' Crédit Mobilier, described by the Legitimist deputy Berryer as 'the greatest gaming house that ever existed', was hampered in obtaining new resources because the government had refused first to allow it to issue its own bonds and then, in 1863, to double its capital. Meanwhile a deflationary trend had begun and the Crédit Mobilier was obliged to advance increasing sums to the companies it had helped to create, in particular to the Société Immobilière, a concern devoted to urban development and reconstruction, especially in Paris and Marseilles. In 1866 the government did consent to the doubling of the Crédit Mobilier's capital, but on conditions which restricted its freedom of action; meanwhile purchasers and tenants for the Société Immobilière's splendid new buildings hung back and by 1867 both companies were in serious difficulties. Before the end of the year the Péreires had to invoke government aid in securing a loan from the Bank of France which would enable them to avoid collapse.

Napoleon, who had supported the Péreires in their early progress, had subsequently remained aloof from their feuds, but the political repercussions of the collapse of so vast an enterprise as the Crédit Mobilier would have been too damaging for the government to ignore its directors' appeal. Rouher, the indefatigable Minister of State, was therefore instructed to do what he could to save them. His task was hard. The Bank of France was naturally a stronghold of orthodoxy and Baron James de Rothschild himself was one of its Regents. Rouher reported to Napoleon that there was 'violent hostility to all the companies created or directed by MM. Péreire on the part of all the financial world apart from the Bank'. These enemies saw their rivals delivered into their hands, and Rouher could not obtain for the Crédit Mobilier a loan of more than half the sum it demanded. The Péreires were forced to resign from both the Crédit Mobilier and the Société Immobilière and new directors acceptable to the Bank were appointed to preside over the gradual liquidation of the Crédit Mobilier.

Thus the fall of the Péreires marked the triumph of orthodoxy and the end of the era of speculative Saint-Simonian finance which had helped to float the Empire on the tide of prosperity. The political opposition rejoiced with the Republican Jules Ferry who declared: 'The year 1867 has begun the liquidation of all the faults of the Second Empire . . . The financial institutions that it had created, cherished, and cosseted with the greatest affection have had the same fate as its diplomacy; after having made much noise in the world, bloated and breathless, they are beginning to faint and fall. The catastrophe of the Crédit Mobilier is the counterpart of the reverses abroad.'

After the Péreires came Haussmann himself, and Ferry, who had stigmatized the Crédit Mobilier, was the author of a work whose title, echoing that of a most popular recent opera, Les Contes d'Hoffmann, was *Les Comptes Fantastiques d'Haussmann*. The prodigious rebuilding of Paris under the direction of the powerful Prefect of the Seine * had entailed a huge and growing expenditure of sums not sanctioned by the Legislative Body or any elected municipal council but obtained by the contractors on advantageous terms from the Crédit Foncier and on conditions which did not comply with the strict letter of the law. Thus, Haussmann's financial methods came in for increasing criticism from those who had led the onslaught against the Péreires and from large sections of the middle classes who preferred an economical government subject to parliamentary control. When the Crédit Foncier in alarm refused further credits, Haussmann had no alternative but to apply to the Legislative Body for support. But his demands were large, and when in 1868 he asked for retrospective approval for a loan of a sum equivalent to a quarter of the whole French budget, the stage was set for a titanic battle. The ensuing debate, which took place in February 1869, was the fiercest of the reign. Once again Rouher was the man who had to stand in the breach and defend a protégé of the Emperor's, but he detested Haussmann and, although he lauded his works, he could not defend his irregularities and admitted that his dealings ought to have had the sanction of the Legislative Body. A loan was finally approved, but Haussmann's position was shaken and the opposition rejoiced at the dissensions in government circles which the affair had revealed on the eve of a general election. Indeed for many, the Emperor himself and his 'system' or lack of it had come under fire.

Everyone knew that 1869 would be a critical year. Since the

last general election in 1863 many new electors had come of
age, who, as Rouher said, did not remember the dangers which
created the Empire—'they have neither our memories nor our
experience'—moreover by-elections had returned mainly
opposition candidates, and the volume of criticism of the
existing system of government and its uncertainties had steadily
grown.* As early as May 1868 a correspondent of the London
house of Rothschild had reported that the government
despaired of success in the next elections, and, as the time for
them drew near, Gambetta, a young Republican of great talent,
predicted that 1869 would be as fatal to the Second Empire
as 1852 had been to the Second Republic.

There was indeed much reason for pessimism among the
supporters of the *status quo*. Apart from the reverses in foreign
policy, the fall of the Péreires, and the discomfiture of Haussmann, Frenchmen were, as the new British Ambassador in
Paris, Lord Lyons, remarked, 'getting tired of so much of the
same thing and want novelty'. Moreover, the government and
the Imperial family itself were subjected to constant attacks
and scurrilous abuse by a newly emancipated press, which had
quickly earned a reputation as one of the most violent and
licentious in the world. In 1852 Victor Hugo had in *Napoléon
le Petit* likened France's ruler to such cruel contemporary
figures as the Neapolitan King Ferdinand or the Austrian
'butcher' of the Hungarians, General Haynau. Now he was
denounced as a modern Tiberius, a Nero or Caligula. Of the
many new papers which indulged in such violence, *La Lanterne*
had by far the greatest circulation on account of its satirical
wit—its definition of France as having 'thirty-six million subjects, not counting the subjects of discontent' was long famous
—but it soon laid itself open to prosecution. Rouher was determined to strike at it hard and its editor, Rochefort, fled to
Brussels for a while to escape the heavy fine imposed by the
courts. Produced for a time in Belgium, the paper did much
less harm. Rouher and his colleague at the Ministry of Justice,
Baroche, were, however, ill-advised in allowing Pinard, the
new Minister of the Interior, to prosecute the editors of three
unimportant Republican papers for organizing a demonstration

* See above, pp. 94–6.

at the tomb of a forgotten Republican deputy, Baudin, who had died on the barricades in December 1851, and for raising a fund to buy him a memorial. The demonstration was insignificant, but the trial gave Gambetta, one of the counsel for the defence, a magnificent opportunity to make a reputation by recalling with extraordinary eloquence the largely forgotten events of 1851 and denouncing the *coup d'état* and its authors. The left-wing papers and speakers took up the cry and Frenchmen were now taught that 'the deliverance of 1851' was in fact a crime and a shame and that the Empire was born of bloodshed. No such public accusations had been heard in France since the Empire began. The legitimacy of the regime itself was openly called into question. In a not dissimilar way the young Louis Napoleon had seized the chance to make political capital out of his own trial after the Boulogne affair in 1840.

The elections of May 1869 were reported to be 'bad' by Napoleon himself to the Empress, who was in Egypt for the opening of the Suez Canal; and 'bad' indeed they were from the point of view of a ruler who was in no haste to 'crown the edifice' with further liberties, however desirable such crowning might still be as an ultimate goal. But they were not, as Gambetta had hoped, fatal to the Empire itself. They were notable as having been freer than any elections since 1849 and as having caused still greater excitement than those of 1863, so much so that in parts of Paris the successes of Republican candidates were followed by some days of riotous demonstration. Moreover, although the government had not abandoned the practice of official candidatures, many of its supporters had preferred to stand as independents, and, while the countryside as a whole still backed the regime as it stood, the opposition groups polled heavily in the towns. Together these groups attracted some 3,300,000 votes compared with approximately 4,500,000 which went to government men. This was a notable advance on the part of the opposition; but it was a triumph not so much for the adherents of the former ruling houses or for the Republicans, who won only 30 out of some 270 seats, as for the moderate men of the various groups who made up what the wits now called the 'Thiers-Parti'. These were men who had supported Thiers's earlier demands for essential liberties and who were willing enough to keep the Emperor, provided he gave them parliamentary government. When the new Legislative Body met they found that they could muster 116 votes and that with Monarchist and Republican support they might even have a majority. Thus the elections served clear notice upon the Emperor to surrender his personal power and, as Persigny told him with the utmost frankness, to change his men as well as his measures.

Napoleon knew well enough that he was beaten, at least for the time being. Indeed he had already been financing out of his private funds a paper which was advocating liberal policies quite at variance with the line sustained by his official spokesmen. Now he quickly adopted the reforming programme of the 116 as his own and sacrificed at last the men who had been the mainstays of his government for the past six years. Recognizing that the position of the now increasingly unpopular Rouher, who was said to be on the way to becoming 'the Guizot of the Empire', was no longer tenable, he allowed him to resign, and with Rouher went Baroche. Men had already commented on the gaps made in the ranks of the Emperor's old supporters: Fortoul, Billault, Morny, all leading ministers, had died before 1866, and Persigny had been virtually disgraced.* Since then Thouvenel, one of the ablest of Napoleon's foreign ministers, Fould and Walewski had also died, the Péreires had fallen, Haussmann had been and still was under attack, and now Rouher and Baroche were sacrificed. More than ever before the Emperor seemed to be alone, a man of 1848, left in isolation to face increasing difficulties and to confront a new generation.

The new liberal concessions announced on July 12 and embodied in a *Sénatus-Consulte* of September 8 marked a decisive step forward. Napoleon now permitted the Legislative Body to share the initiative in legislation, to elect its own officers, to amend government bills, to vote the budget clause by clause, to have still greater freedom to question ministers, and to consider tariff changes. The long heralded era of the Liberal Empire was near at hand and, as a further mark of his readiness to break with the past, Napoleon granted a general

* See above, p. 89.

amnesty which eventually included once celebrated Republican figures such as Ledru-Rollin as well as more recent exiles such as Rochefort.

But, as usual, Napoleon hurried slowly. The caretaker government which succeeded Rouher's was not drawn from the Third Party, and the Legislative Body was prorogued for four and a half months. Moreover, in August and early September Napoleon had a severe bout of illness which incapacitated him for a while, caused a slump on the Bourse, and even gave rise to rumours that he was about to abdicate. Eventually, after his recovery, he selected as the man to head his first true cabinet not Thiers, who by virtue of his experience and his leading role in the last parliament might have seemed the obvious choice, but the much younger and comparatively inexperienced Émile Ollivier. There were, however, good reasons for this preference. Thiers, the man who in Louis Philippe's day had enunciated the doctrine that 'the king reigns but does not govern', was too dominating a character for Napoleon's taste. Moreover, as a rabid protectionist, a man who had little if any interest in social questions or sympathy for the cause of nationalities, Thiers in many ways epitomized a narrow conservative middle-class outlook which was the antithesis of the Emperor's visionary idealism. Napoleon had no intention of being relegated to the position of a 'roi fainéant' and, though he could charm Ollivier, it is doubtful whether he could have charmed Thiers into docility. In Ollivier, on the other hand, he found a man already designated by Morny, a high-minded idealist with whom he had much in common, a man who had played a prominent part in parliament for more than a decade and who also, though in a very different way from Thiers, typified some of the bourgeois aspirations of the time. He could work with Ollivier and hope to manage him as he was never likely to succeed in managing Thiers. Thus, after lengthy negotiations, Ollivier was summoned to a secret meeting with the Emperor at Compiègne one November night and bidden to envelop his head in a muffler in order 'to pass without being noticed'. The eventual upshot was the cabinet of January 2, 1870, which marks the real beginning of the Liberal Empire.

Even its engendering thus took place in that atmosphere of conspiracy which Napoleon still so dearly loved.

The formation of Ollivier's cabinet, which, in Napoleon's own words, was to be 'homogeneous' and faithfully represent the majority in the Legislative Body, did indeed mark the 'crowning of the edifice' at long last. It gave the country after eighteen years the novelty of something at last akin to parliamentarism. A long period of uncertainty was at an end. A rise in government funds reflected a new confidence. And this confidence seemed to be shared by the Emperor himself. Once he had resolved his hesitations, as on many occasions before, he showed a new cheerfulness and sense of relief, remarking at his New Year reception that 'When a traveller after a long journey sheds part of his burden, it gives him fresh strength to continue his march'. His calmness, too, astonished observers. 'Here', noted one of them, Ludovic Halévy, 'is a man who six months ago . . . had France in his hand . . . He has tranquilly let everything go . . . His intimates are in consternation, the Empress is angry. Around him the Emperor sees none but anxious and gloomy faces. "What's wrong with you", he says . . . "things have never been so peaceful during a revolution." ' Napoleon had indeed some reason for satisfaction. Men in all parties were found to hail a change which the *Revue des Deux Mondes* described as 'if not the greatest of all revolutions . . . one of the most interesting . . . most salutary and most opportune'. He had triumphantly accomplished that most difficult of all political manoeuvres, the peaceful transformation of an authoritarian into a liberal regime.

Moreover, ill though he often was, his hand had not lost its cunning and he had not, as Ludovic Halévy suggested, 'let everything go'. He might let his 'homogeneous' cabinet of 'honest men', as one of them claimed they were, dismiss Haussmann, set up commissions of enquiry into such problems as decentralization, technical education, and 'social peace', establish a Ministry of Fine Arts, and in general embark upon a further programme of liberal reforms; but he had no intention of abdicating and releasing his grip upon what he regarded as the essentials of power. He himself had appointed the Ministers of War and Marine, and in his chief minister Ollivier he had, he told the Austrian Ambassador, a man who had 'two precious qualities which make me forget his failings. He believes in me and is the eloquent interpreter of my ideas, especially when I let him think they are his own.' Nowhere was it more important for Napoleon that his own ideas should be adequately reflected than in the making and remaking of the constitution itself, and this became a major question in the spring of 1870.

Men might speak of the Liberal Empire as a return to parliamentary government, but in fact it was a parliamentarism of a distinctly restricted type which may, it has been suggested, find its place in a 'tradition which can be traced through modern French history, from 1815, 1848, 1870 to 1958'. This was not only because of the authority still retained by the Emperor under the *Sénatus-Consulte* of September 1869—for instance by the article declaring that 'the ministers depend only upon the Emperor'—but also because the constitution that followed the *Sénatus-Consulte* in May 1870 was a hybrid structure which admirably conformed to the great Napoleon's dictum that a constitution should be short and obscure. It may be wondered whether his nephew, who had known how to profit from the defects of the constitution of 1848, did not deliberately favour such obscurities, while encouraging his chief minister to believe that they happily embodied his own preference for a 'mixed' form of constitutional government. In the event, the new constitution combined parliamentary government through responsible ministers with limited monarchy and also with rule by an emperor who was still commander-in-chief of the armed forces, had the right to declare war and conclude peace treaties, and was responsible to the people, 'to whom he always has the right of appeal'.

This last element was no doubt the most important of all, from Napoleon's point of view. The idea of a new constitution had been forced upon Ollivier by the desire of certain deputies to alter the existing arrangements for amending the constitution and to transfer this power from the Senate to the Legislative Body. But, when the new constitution was made public, it was seen that, while the Senate was transformed into an upper house with the right to initiate and alter legislation, the constitution itself could 'only be modified by the People, upon the initiative of the Emperor'. In other words, Napoleon, perhaps influenced by the President of the Senate, none other than his former henchman Rouher, had skilfully reintroduced the characteristically Bonapartist device of a recourse to a plebiscite. Moreover, he also persuaded his ministers that the constitutional changes should be submitted to popular approval. In a speech at Lyons in September 1852 he had spoken of 'the Emperor Napoleon I three times chosen by the people'. Was not this an admirable opportunity for the Emperor's nephew also to profit from a third plebiscite, strengthening the prospects of his dynasty, and reserving the future?

The plebiscite of May 8 which invited the French people to approve the liberal reforms of the constitution effected by the Emperor since 1860 and to modify the new constitution of 1870 showed that Napoleon's judgment was not at fault. The voters who wrote 'Oui' numbered over 7,300,000; those who wrote 'Non' only some 1,570,000. Even allowing for the facts that the big towns once again voted with the opposition and that there were nearly 1,900,000 abstentions, the vote was a massive verdict in favour of the regime.

But the liberal reforms of the new ministry were never completed. The outbreak of war in July 1870 and the collapse of the Empire itself in September were to leave a great question-mark for ever poised over the last phase of Napoleonic government and over the significance of the plebiscite itself. If it was a verdict in favour of the regime, men might still question which kind of empire it supported. Was it primarily a vote of approval for liberalism or was it rather a renewed vote of confidence in the Emperor himself, regardless of the form of his government? And how would Napoleon himself interpret it? Did it mean that he would regard it as a definitive endorsement of his liberalism, and that he would abide by the new constitution and liberal programmes, believing them to be fundamental for the stability of the Empire and the security of the dynasty, or did it mean that he would consider them as a temporary expedient, to be borne with for a while, as he had borne with the constitution of the Second Republic, and then to be cast aside as opportunity occurred?

We shall never know the answer. Probably it was unknown to Napoleon himself, who was above all an opportunist, feeling his way and sounding 'la force des choses'. On the one hand, there is little doubt that the Empress and the authoritarian Bonapartists detested the new arrangements and would gladly have induced him to revert to an authoritarian system. Had there been new outbreaks of violence, had there been attempts at insurrection by the more extreme Republicans and by members of the Socialist International, whose numbers in France were rapidly growing, it is not inconceivable that the reactionaries might have persuaded him that the chance had come to pose once again as the saviour of society and return to 1851-2. Yet his memory of the *coup d'état* was not a happy one and, unless he were to relapse into being a mere instrument of the authoritarians, it is unlikely that an ailing but still astute man in his sixties would have adopted such a course unless he saw in it the only hope of saving the regime and dynasty. Moreover, the advent of the Liberal Empire had at last begun to win for Napoleon the support of many of the intellectuals and middle classes who had hitherto remained aloof, and in Alsace there were signs that even the workers were beginning to think of the government as on their side against close-fisted employers. Here were portents which Napoleon III, who had extolled Napoleon I as a 'plebeian Emperor' welcoming all classes, was unlikely to ignore. It is to be remembered, too, that the new constitution gave him considerable power, especially in those departments of war and diplomacy which he had always made peculiarly his own, and that he had not lost his skill in handling politicians. The Ollivier ministry might not in any event have lasted long, but, once the plebiscite had convinced them that the Empire was there to stay, there would have been plenty of other deputies to be tempted by the lure of office. One day, perhaps, who knows but that the father of the opportunist party of the Third Republic, Gambetta himself, might have served that other great opportunist, Napoleon III, in fruitful partnership? The Emperor, who believed in marching with events, would surely not easily have been persuaded to overthrow the edifice he had so recently crowned and to replace it by some more anachronistic structure.

But it was events of a very different kind from the holding of equivocal plebiscites and the voting of equivocal constitutions that were to determine that the young Prince Imperial would never reign as Napoleon IV. In June 1870 the political skies seemed unusually clear—there was peace abroad and relative peace at home—but early in July a small black cloud appeared suddenly on the southern horizon. This foreran a tempest which, raging more swiftly and dramatically than anyone dreamed, tossed Napoleon aside and swept the Second Empire to its destruction.

Chapter Ten

The Defences, the Hohenzollern Crisis, and the Débâcle

IN an arresting passage of *Des Idées Napoléoniennes* Louis Napoleon had imagined his uncle's angered shade roused in its heavenly abode by the agitations and judgments of mortal men and answering those who accused him by putting to them a series of questions. Among them were the following: 'Have you secured for France allies on whom she can count in the day of danger?' and 'Have you organized the national guard in such a manner that it will be an invincible barrier against invasion?' Thirty-four years later we may picture the great Napoleon's shade aroused again, this time to welcome his nephew to the Elysian fields and also to demand from him an account of his stewardship. What would Napoleon III have replied to these self-same questions? His answers must have been embarrassed and faltering: 'Sire, I tried, but the difficulties were great. I tried, but did not succeed.'

Sadowa had made Frenchmen see in Prussia an enemy for the first time since 1815, and the subsequent reverses of French diplomacy, culminating in the Luxemburg affair, destroyed any valid hopes of restored Franco-German friendship for more than eighty years. The ease with which Prussia had defeated Austria showed that she was likely to be a formidable foe, and the way in which she had exploited Napoleon's diplomatic blunders to bind the South German states to her in time of war had, by the spring of 1867, made it clear that war with Prussia might well be war with the whole of Germany. In such circumstances it was elementary prudence for Napoleon to seek on the one hand to ensure that France should not be friendless and on the other to strengthen her defences.

The obvious ally against Prussia was Austria, who was still smarting from her defeat and whose Minister for Foreign Affairs, the Saxon Count Beust, was a firm opponent of Bismarck. But Napoleon, never an Austrophil, disliked the idea of an alliance which would appear to disavow all his previous policies as a champion of nationality. He had rejected the idea before peace had been concluded and had then turned to Prussia direct.* When the Prussian negotiations went to earth he tried first to renew the old *entente* with Russia on the basis of an understanding in the Near East. But no real basis of co-operation could be found, since France was preoccupied by the situation in Western Europe, which she wished to redress to her own advantage, whereas Russia did not fear Prussia and, as at the time of the later Franco-Russian alliance in the 1890s, wanted French support for her own policies in the East. Moreover, France had no wish to accelerate the break-up of Turkey, whereas Russia hoped to profit by its disintegration. Thus the negotiations were in the end abortive.

It was the Luxemburg crisis in the spring of 1867 which sharply accentuated the danger of war with Prussia and caused Napoleon to turn to Austria in earnest. Henceforward, the Austrian alliance, hitherto avoided or half-heartedly pursued, was the main objective of his policy. But it was an elusive goal. Not only was Austria traditionally cautious and slow, but she was in little condition to face another war so soon. Moreover, reorganized as the result of her defeats, she was in 1867 in the process of becoming the Dual Monarchy of Austria-Hungary. This meant that Hungarian influence over the policies of Vienna was increasingly important, and the Hungarians, as Napoleon was anxiously aware, distrusted Russia far more than Prussia.

Thus, when, in the spring of 1867, Napoleon offered Austria an offensive and defensive alliance against Prussia and proposed that in the event of victory France should obtain the left bank of the Rhine while Austria should regain Silesia (which Frederick the Great had seized from her in the eighteenth century) and re-establish her influence in Southern Germany, Beust was not to be seduced. For one thing, he pointed out that

* See above, p. 144.

the ten million Germans in Austria would have little enthusiasm for a war, one of whose main objects would be to
transfer German territory to France. For another, he feared the
reactions of Russia. Beust then, for all his dislike of Bismarck,
was inclined to accept the German settlement and regard
Austria's exclusion from Germany as final. He looked for
Austrian expansion in the Balkans rather than in Germany and
suggested that France should first of all back Vienna's aims in
this direction. Not unnaturally Napoleon hesitated to do so,
for Austria's chief rival in the Balkans was Russia: were an
Austrian advance in this region to provoke Russia to war,
Austria would be fully engaged and his main objective,
Austria's help against Prussia, would not be attained.

The idea of an alliance, however, continued to attract both
Paris and Vienna, and, at a meeting with Francis Joseph at
Salzburg in August 1867, Napoleon, perhaps genuinely unable
to believe that Austria had resigned herself for good to the loss
of her position in Germany, renewed his earlier proposals in a
modified form, suggesting that France should gain only the
Saar district and Austria Southern Silesia. But these suggestions,
too, were rejected by Beust, and so the negotiations relapsed
into the acceptance of an ill-defined *entente*. In 1869, however, they entered a new phase with the suggestion, readily
accepted by Napoleon, that instead of a dual there should be a
triple alliance, with Italy as the third partner. For Austria the
advantage would be that in a war with Prussia she would no
longer have to fear an attack from the south by Italy, who
coveted the Trentino, while Italy hoped by entering upon such
negotiations to obtain either the Trentino or Rome or both.

It was Rome, however, that once again proved a main
stumbling-block. Rome had been evacuated by French troops
in December 1866.* But shortly before, Napoleon had admitted
to Cowley that his position there was 'detestable. For 18 years
I have been the Pope's mainstay and now I have the appearance of abandoning him. If anything was to go wrong I should
be obliged to go to his help. Provided I could clear out on the
following day.' Something did go wrong and within less than
a year, for on October 23, 1867, Garibaldian forces invaded

* See above, pp. 104–5.

Papal territory. Napoleon, who could not afford to alienate French Catholic opinion afresh, felt obliged to go once more to the aid of Pius IX. The obligation was the more irksome because, as the British representative in Rome later remarked, throughout the long period of French occupation the Pope had 'systematically disregarded and despised the advice of his protectors' and refused to reform his government. Nevertheless, French forces were hastily despatched again to Rome and, armed with new *chassepots* or breech-loading rifles, which their commander declared to have 'done wonders', routed the Garibaldians at Mentana on November 3. In a maladroit speech in the Legislative Body, defending the French action, Rouher declared that Italy should 'never' take possession of Rome: 'France will never tolerate such a violation of her honour.' The Emperor, who was only too eager 'to clear out on the following day', thus found it impossible to withdraw, and once again a French garrison was installed on Papal territory, at Città Vecchia. He wisely told his minister that in politics men should never say 'never'; but the Catholics were triumphant and he did not disown Rouher as he had disowned Drouyn de Lhuys in 1866.

Thus the Roman question was an obvious card for Italy to play when her alliance was sought. At first all seemed to go well with negotiations for an arrangement between France, Austria and Italy. This was, however, to be an agreement far more limited in scope than the alliance with Austria at which Napoleon had originally aimed. It was not even an alliance, for, while the three powers agreed not to negotiate with others without informing one another, they proposed to conclude an alliance only if and when a general war broke out. Moreover, their agreement on a mutual guarantee of existing territories barred the way to Italy's aspirations in the Trentino and made it all the more certain that she would try to settle the Roman question to her advantage. This she did in June 1869, expressing her readiness to accept the proposed treaty, provided that Napoleon at once withdrew his troops from Papal territory and undertook to interfere no more in the Roman question, and provided also that France and Austria agreed not to undo the German settlement of 1866. These conditions were quite unacceptable to Napoleon, who dared not perform a fresh *volte-face* over Rome and could hardly, in view of anti-Prussian feeling in France, forgo any chance of exploiting the German situation to French and Austrian advantage should the allies be victorious in a general war.

Thus, once again divergent interests produced a deadlock. It was not, however, complete. Relations between the three powers continued friendly, and in September 1869 their monarchs exchanged letters which at least kept alive the notion of an eventual alliance. Yet the fact remained that after two and a half years of negotiation with Austria and six months of negotiation with Italy, Napoleon had not obtained a binding promise of aid from either. In the exchange of letters in September Victor Emmanuel had reiterated his inability to sign a treaty so long as French troops remained on Roman soil and, although Napoleon had assured Francis Joseph that, were his dominions threatened by aggression, he 'would not hesitate for a moment to place all the French forces' on his side, Francis Joseph's reply contained no similar assurance of Austro-Hungarian aid in the event of aggression against France. Austria continued to fear Russia, and her fears were constantly played upon by Bismarck, ever watchful in the background. All that Napoleon could hope for and perhaps delude himself into believing was that, when a crisis came, the three powers would feel morally bound to come to one another's aid.

It was, however, to Napoleon's credit that he did not abandon his attempts to win greater security for France. No sooner had the September exchanges made clear that nothing further was to be gained for the time being from Austria or Italy than he turned again to Russia, sending a new ambassador, Fleury, with instructions to sound the Russian Government as to the feasibility of an *entente*, not this time to overthrow the 1866 German settlement, but to preserve it against further Prussian expansion. Fleury, however, soon saw that he could get nowhere. This was with good reason, for, unknown to France and Austria, the Tsar had in March 1868 promised Prussia that in the event of a Franco-Prussian war he would restrain Austria by mobilizing 100,000 men and placing them on the Austrian frontier. Russia, in fact, hoped that a war in the west in which she was not involved would give her the long-looked-for opportunity to undo the Treaty of Paris of 1856. The opportunity was to come sooner than she or anyone else expected.

Thus, baulked in all directions, knowing that it was useless to approach England who had no army to speak of, whose governments stood increasingly aloof from European affairs, and whose suspicions he had recently aroused anew in the Belgian railways affair, Napoleon could only seize what opportunities might still present themselves to strengthen his ties with Austria. In March 1870, unknown to his new Ministers of War and Foreign Affairs, he engaged the Inspector-General of the Austrian army, the Archduke Albrecht, who was visiting Paris, in secret military talks with a view to combining Austrian and French movements in case of war, and in June he sent General Lebrun to Vienna to continue the conversations. They were not, however, to be the fruitful preliminaries of a definite alliance, as were the later military talks with Russia in the 1890s or with England before the First World War. They were still, as the Archduke said, 'academic'; and when war came suddenly in July France was to wage it alone.

All Napoleon's efforts had been fruitless. In a world of *Realpolitik* no feeling of moral obligation was compulsive enough to bring Austria and Italy immediately to his side. When war was certain and the Austro-Hungarian government had refused his appeal for aid there could be little hope that Italy would come to his assistance. Her army was weak, her government was beset by internal problems, and she still demanded Rome to which Napoleon still desperately clung. It was incidentally ironical that one of the arguments against intervention which had prevailed at Vienna was that of the Hungarian, Andrassy, who pointed out that Napoleon had never pursued a grand objective to the end. All his enterprises had stopped short of their goal: therefore, if Austria-Hungary entered the war on France's side she would risk being left in the lurch like Sardinia at Villafranca!

If France was to meet Prussia without any certainty of allies it was all the more incumbent upon her to ensure that her army was ready for any emergency. Of this Napoleon was well aware, and so, simultaneously with his search for allies he launched a programme of army reform. In the La Valette circular of September 18, 1866, he had inserted a passage which declared 'the necessity for the defence of our territory of perfecting our military organization without delay. The nation will not fail in this duty which can be a threat to no one.' Frenchmen thus received a first warning that the time was at hand when they should be ready to make sacrifices in order to meet any danger from the east.

The French army, of which Napoleon III was constitution-ally Commander-in-Chief, was organized in accordance with two fundamental military laws, the Law Gouvion St. Cyr of 1818 and the Law Soult which modified it in 1832. Conscription, intensely unpopular during the Napoleonic wars, had been abolished in 1814 and the army, as subsequently re-fashioned, was to all intents and purposes a professional force. Since, how-ever, the number of volunteers was inadequate to make up the full peace-time complement, conscription had returned in a diluted form and under another name. Every Frenchman on reaching the age of twenty was theoretically liable to serve in an annual levy, the size of which after 1830 was fixed from year to year by parliament. Who should in fact serve was determined by drawing lots. Thus all were nominally equal before the law. But in practice a number of young men were for various reasons exempted from service, while those who drew a 'bad number'—a misfortune against which they could insure as against fire or hail—could pay for a substitute. The men finally selected were liable to serve for seven years, but by no means all did so because, largely for reasons of economy, the annual contingent was divided into two, only the first part being called upon to serve the full term, and the second and larger part being sent home on leave unless or until required.

As an opponent of the July Monarchy, Louis Napoleon had been a severe critic of this system and contrasted it un-favourably with the Prussian. As early as 1833 he had urged the Swiss to model their system of defence upon the Prussian

Landwehr, or citizen militia, which formed a territorial reserve. Ten years later, in *Le Progrès du Pas-de-Calais*, he had correctly foretold that the Prussian system would 'inevitably be adopted by all the continental powers because it responds to the new demands of the people of Europe'. In Prussia, he had explained, all men between the ages of 20 and 40 were liable to three years' active service. They then spent two years in the reserve, after which they were enrolled in the separate Landwehr. In his view, this system solved the problem of finding a method of organization 'which in the hour of danger provides thousands of trained men and which in peace time is a small burden on the budget and takes few young men away from agriculture'. Moreover, unlike the French National Guard, a purely bourgeois levy, the Landwehr was a truly citizen force: indeed the Prussian system 'destroyed all barriers between the citizen and soldier' and elevated every man's feelings 'by making him understand that the defence of his country was his foremost duty'. It was France's duty to 'organize her forces in such a way as to shield her for ever from invasion'. He would have liked to have seen the abolition of the practice of buying substitutes, the creation of a strong reserve, and the conversion of the National Guard into a real territorial army. The Prussian system he had roundly praised as 'the finest military organization that has ever existed among civilized nations'.

It might thus have been expected that, once he was in power, one of Napoleon III's foremost aims would have been a thorough-going reform of the army. Yet by 1866 only two small modifications had been introduced. The practice of hiring substitutes had grown between 1824 and 1851 and was increasingly subject to abuse and therefore to criticism. Accordingly, by a law of 1855, it was replaced by a system under which those who were called up but did not wish to serve could buy exemption by contributing to a central fund. This fund enabled the government to fill the gap by re-engaging discharged men who were willing to serve a further term. The second modification, introduced in 1859 at the Emperor's instigation, was that henceforward the men in the second portion of the annual contingent were required to undergo a progressively diminishing period of annual training.

The reasons why Napoleon III did not attempt any more drastic reform, despite his earlier criticisms of the existing system, can only be guessed at. He had proclaimed that the Empire spelt peace, so that the introduction of a system partly designed to increase the size of the effective army might well have been misinterpreted and have aroused widespread suspicion both at home and abroad. He had many other preoccupations, and when he did go to war in Europe his armies had been victorious. France, therefore, was still universally considered the foremost military power and there was no reason for Frenchmen not to regard their military system as fully adequate to their country's needs. It was a system which admirably suited the richer classes, who could purchase exemption, and the majority of the military leaders themselves, scornful of new methods and theories, were complacently content, sharing the belief that the French army was the finest in the world, and despising the short-term conscript militia forces of countries such as Switzerland and Prussia. Thus Napoleon himself may well have accepted the view that, despite many defects of which he could not but be aware, the existing system was sufficient for his immediate purposes.

Yet it is a grave criticism of his direction of affairs that he did not take action before the shock of Sadowa brought home the urgency of reform. Apart from the administrative muddles which had characterized both the Crimean and the Italian campaigns, the Italian war had demonstrated a shortage of effective manpower. The army had sufficed for the war in the peninsula, but it had not been possible to organize another force at home to combat the Prussian threat on the Rhine. Yet this warning went unheeded. In consequence, in the crucial days after Sadowa, it was found that, out of a nominal strength of 654,000 men, only 250,000 active soldiers were immediately available. Rome, Algeria and Mexico required nearly 100,000; the first contingent of 1865 was not yet trained; the pitifully small reserve of 27,000 was also unready; and 110,000 others for various reasons had to be written off as non-combatants. Meanwhile the Prussian army, under the direction of General von Roon, firmly supported by the King and Bismarck, had undergone a reform which was to make of it a still larger and more efficient fighting force. The period of service in the regular reserve had been increased: men were to pass into the Landwehr only after having served with the colours or reserve for seven years; and the Landwehr itself was brought under closer control by the regular army in such a way as to make it tantamount to a second line reserve. Thus the strength of the regular army was considerably increased, while the Landwehr became a more effective force. After 1866, the Prussian system was extended to the whole North German Confederation, whose army strength in 1870 was reckoned at about 730,000 men excluding the Landwehr. This force was the more formidable because during the previous decade another general, Moltke, had been shaping for it an admirable directing organization in the highly trained Prussian General Staff, compared with which, it has been said, the General Staffs of other armies were mere collections of adjutants and clerks to aid the commander in the field.

The Prussian army reforms had, however, been put through at the price of a great constitutional struggle. The people, and especially the Liberals, were content with and proud of their Landwehr as it stood, and, for all their military traditions, saw no reason to submit to the new and more onerous service. When the House of Deputies refused to vote the additional funds to pay for a larger army, the King, first and foremost a soldier, had dissolved it, only to be confronted by a new house equally hostile. He had at first contemplated abdicating rather than abandon the reforms, and had then fallen back upon Bismarck, who had proved to be the strong man he needed and had ridden roughshod over the lower house until the army's brilliant successes in war had come to vindicate his master's programme. Thus, when Napoleon at last turned to the idea of large-scale reform, he had before him a very recent example of the passionate opposition that proposals to increase the size of an army could arouse and of the ruthlessness which it might be necessary to exercise if such proposals were to be carried through unchanged.

How far, if at all, it influenced his conduct is uncertain. But his own position was in some ways weaker than that of the Prussian King. Whereas in Prussia the dynasty was securely established, in France the regime itself might be jeopardized by a conflict of such gravity. In Prussia, too, the ablest military men wholeheartedly supported the King, whereas in France the reactions of the military leaders to Napoleon's reforming programme were very mixed. Thus the Emperor, who in any case was not a soldier like the King of Prussia, was not prepared to stake everything on the success of his measures, and though at one time he contemplated dissolving the Legislative Body he thought better of such a move. The Prussian precedent was certainly not encouraging and he had no Bismarck to fall back upon.

Once he had recovered from his illness after the Sadowa crisis Napoleon lost little time in tackling the problem of army reform. He put forward different plans in September and October, both of which aimed at an army of a million men. In the first, the most conspicuous feature was the constitution, alongside the active army and reserves of 600,000 men, of a kind of counterpart of the Prussian Landwehr, a Garde Nationale Mobile, in which service would be compulsory and which would be commanded by regular soldiers and undergo an annual period of training. In the second, he returned to his earlier idea of general compulsory service (he had his articles of the 'forties reprinted at this time in various newspapers) but allowed the purchase of exemption after three years' service.

These projects initiated a period of discussion, proposal and counter-proposal which continued for sixteen months, during which the original schemes were continually modified and weakened. At first Napoleon had hoped to secure endorsement of his main ideas by a specially appointed commission of military men and civilian ministers, but since it could reach no conclusion he disbanded it, replaced the unco-operative War Minister, Randon, by a more enlightened soldier, Marshal Niel, and in conjunction with him elaborated a new programme, which he had published in the *Moniteur* on December 12. This aimed at a total force of 1,232,000. 160,000 men were to be called up each year and be liable for six years' service either in the active army, which would total 417,000, or in the reserve of 425,000. Their six years over, they would be required to serve for another three in the Garde Mobile which, however, could be called up only by a special law and which would need little additional exercise since it was already comprised of trained men. The Garde Mobile would provide a territorial reserve of 330,000 men.

Publication in the *Moniteur* was a well-tried means of testing public reactions. Unfortunately they were highly unfavourable. The whole of the press was loud in its criticisms. The government, by trying to justify the Emperor's policy with regard to the German question and by expressing satisfaction with the new situation in Europe, had cut the ground from under its own feet. Frenchmen did not see why there was any need for such drastic measures. The fixing of the annual contingent at 160,000 was denounced as unconstitutional, since it deprived the Legislative Body of its control, and the discretionary powers left to the Emperor aroused fears of new adventures overseas. These criticisms, reinforced by a spate of pamphlets, provoked widespread uneasiness and, most disquieting of all, the reports of prefects and other officials in the departments indicated that, apart from the conservative middle-classes whose opposition was to be expected, it was the peasantry, the main support of the regime, who were most deeply disturbed. Under these circumstances, it was no wonder that most deputies, with a general election ahead of them in 1869, were in no mind to risk their seats by championing so unpopular a measure. When the bill, already further modified by the Conseil d'État, went before the Legislative Body in the spring of 1867 it emerged emasculated beyond recognition. Recognizing his defeat, the Emperor withdrew it and in a brief visit to the northern departments in August made no reference to the need for sacrifices. In November a new bill was put forward which, after further debates, became law in February 1868. Even this, a simulacrum of Niel's original proposals, met with opposition.

Thus the government had given way on one point after another, and the law as finally voted preserved many of the weaknesses of the old system. Only part of the reserve was to receive any appreciable training, and the Garde Mobile, which was to consist of all men of military age who had purchased exemption, was to undergo an annual training of only two weeks. Moreover, the enrolment of even this attenuated force caused serious disturbances in Toulouse and elsewhere. In consequence, the regular soldiers refused to take it seriously and, when war came, Niel's successor, Leboeuf, had done nothing to ensure that the Garde Mobile, by which the Emperor had set such store, was organized, equipped or trained. It could not conceivably be 'the invincible barrier against invasion' that the great Napoleon's shade had desired. The final tragedy of this sorry failure, for which ruler and ruled were alike responsible, was that the country as a whole, quite unable to follow the technicalities of the prolonged discussions of 1866–8, fondly believed that it now had the trained army of 1,200,000 men which the Emperor had proclaimed as his objective. It was soon to make the bitter discovery that it had been living in a paradise of fools.

'It is Spain's fate always to be our undoing'. Never were these words of D'Argenson to be proved more dramatically true than in 1870. The drama was the greater because Spain, immersed in her own turbulent concerns, had played but a peripheral part in the history of the Second Empire. France's fierce struggle with England for dynastic influence in the peninsula had died down before the fall of the July Monarchy and good relations with Spain had been strengthened by Napoleon III's marriage and only slightly impaired by the Mexican affair. But in 1868 the Bourbon queen, Isabella II, was driven from her throne and fled to France. A new dynastic struggle in Spain was about to begin.

The Spanish revolution was regarded with misgiving by Napoleon, for it gave rise to talk of a Republic or of an Orleanist king in the person of the Duc de Montpensier, Louis Philippe's youngest son, either of which solutions must be unpalatable to a Bonaparte with Orleanist and Republican enemies at home. But the Republican danger was averted when in May 1869 the Cortes voted for a monarchy, while Montpensier's prospects were reduced by the opposition to him of the leading member of the Spanish provisional government, Marshal Prim. A king, however, had yet to be found and, apart from Montpensier, the most likely candidates were not tempted by the uneasy glitter of the Spanish crown. Unable to find a suitable Spanish or Portuguese prince or princess, Prim and his friends had to look further afield.

As one of the few eligible Catholic princes outside the peninsula, Leopold, Prince of Hohenzollern-Sigmaringen, was frequently mentioned. Apart from his personal qualities and suitable age, he had the advantage of a Portuguese wife and kinship with Napoleon III as well as the Prussian royal house. But he was a wholly German prince in upbringing and outlook, and when the rumours of his candidature reached Paris they caused disquiet. Napoleon himself early in 1869 said that he could tolerate Montpensier if the worst came to the worst, since his election to the throne would be anti-dynastic only, a blow to the Bonapartes, but that the choice of Leopold would be intolerable, since it would be an affront to France herself. Accordingly, the French Ambassador in Berlin had been instructed to mention the rumours to Bismarck and to discover the Prussian government's reactions. Bismarck was mild and friendly in his reply. He did not conceal that he had discussed the matter with the King of Prussia and with Leopold's father, Prince Karl Anton, but he expressed the view that the Spanish crown was an uncomfortable one and that it was therefore highly unlikely that either the King or Karl Anton would encourage Leopold to accept it should it be offered.

There the matter rested for the time being. Two months earlier, in a despatch to the North German envoy at St. Petersburg concerning the possibility of a war involving Russia as well as France, Bismarck had written: 'We would try to create a situation which would force France to attack, or, at least, threaten Germany. Mobilization, national manifestations in Germany and Italy, our relations with Belgium or even with Spain, would give us the opportunity of a diversion which would bring us into the war without giving the appearance of an aggressive . . . war'. Bismarck himself had added the reference to Spain, but, although he was watching the Spanish situation with interest and was anxious to strengthen Prussian influence in Madrid, there is no convincing evidence that he was already setting a trap for France or that the Hohenzollern candidature had his active support before the end of February 1870.

By then the situation had developed. The Ollivier government had come to power in France, and Bismarck, although well aware that French policies were unpredictable, was inclined to think that its advent improved his chances of completing German unification without the need for war. Ollivier himself sought through England to initiate talks on disarmament; he was well-disposed towards German aspirations and had made it clear that he would not oppose the union of North and South if this was the German people's will. The country was already united militarily and commercially: what remained to be done, he said, was 'purely Prussia's business and it will bring more difficulties than strength'. But Ollivier, liberal though he was, was convinced also of the importance of being firm at home and abroad. At home he had not hesitated to arrest a number of leaders of the International or to call out cavalry to check a potentially dangerous demonstration organized by the extreme Left on the occasion of the funeral of a journalist, who had been shot dead by an obscure member of the Bonaparte family. Abroad he was as anxious as any patriotic Frenchman that France should not have to bow her head to further humiliations—indeed Lord Lyons on January 30 reported him as saying that a public rebuff from Prussia would be fatal – ' "un échec . . . c'est la guerre!" Those who had to render an account to Parliament and the country were less able than the former Government to put up with any wound to the national pride . . . they must show firmness, or they would not be able to cope with Revolution and Socialism at home.' In Spain, meanwhile, the search for a king was hardly any further advanced, for Prim's efforts to promote the candidature of the Duke of Genoa, a Harrow schoolboy and nephew of Victor Emmanuel, had also fallen through by the end of December 1869. An unofficial but not wholly unpromising approach had, however, been made to Leopold and his father in September, and since, of the candidates still left in the field, Leopold seemed the most promising, Prim decided to approach him officially.

It was now that Bismarck took a direct hand for the first time. When he saw that Prim was serious, Bismarck, too, became serious and perceived the advantage Leopold's acceptance might have for Prussia in terms of prestige and strategy. On the one hand, the Hohenzollerns would 'gain an esteem and an exalted position in the world such as does not find its analogy in the past record of the Hapsburgs since Charles V'; on the other, in a war between France and Germany, France would have to keep at least one army corps on the Spanish frontier. But the King, 'utterly against the affair,' was unmoved by Bismarck's arguments, and Leopold, though ready to make 'the sacrifice' on certain conditions, would do so only at the King's command. By May 4 it looked as though 'the affair' was at an end. Prim, however, under increasing pressure from deputies impatient at the long delay in finding a monarch, would not take 'no' for an answer, while Bismarck at last succeeded in persuading Karl Anton that it was vital to the German interest that his son should accept the proffered crown. On June 21 William I gave his reluctant consent. Prim's elated envoy telegraphed at once to Madrid, where the Cortes were at the end of their session, to say that he was bringing the good news of Leopold's acceptance and hoped to be back 'about the 26th.' The plan was that, provided he announced his return for before July 1, the Cortes would be held together, told of Leopold's acceptance and conditions, and proceed to his election.

No such momentous secret could be kept for four months. The news was out in Madrid on July 1, set Paris agog on the evening of the 2nd, and was officially confirmed by telegram from the French Embassy in Madrid on the 3rd. Meanwhile the political and diplomatic world in Germany had gone on holiday. King William was taking a cure at Ems, the French Ambassador at another spa, Leopold was in the Alps, and Bismarck, who had retired to Varzin in Pomerania, took the line that the affair was nothing to do with the Prussian government but concerned only Spain and the Hohenzollerns. The great question was what would be the French reaction. Napoleon III and his ministers were understandably astonished and dismayed. They were convinced that their position would be untenable if Leopold were allowed to rule in Spain, since

French opinion would not tolerate another humiliation at Prussia's hands. They therefore launched a full-scale diplomatic offensive to try and secure his withdrawal, making it clear that, if they did not succeed, war was bound to result. Napoleon himself sent messages to the King of the Belgians and to Gladstone. His foreign minister asked the British and Italian governments to use their influence at Madrid. A direct approach was made to the Spanish Regent, and representations were made through the normal channels to the Prussian and Spanish governments. But the key persons in the crisis were the King of Prussia and, since Leopold himself was 'most unaccountably' lost in the Alps, Leopold's father Karl Anton. King William was gravely disturbed by the reports from Paris and by the urgent representations made to him direct by the French Ambassador, Benedetti, and decided that Leopold's withdrawal would be desirable if it could be effected without pressure from him. Karl Anton, for his part, was shaken by the gloomy warnings of Olozaga, the Spanish Ambassador in Paris, who disliked the candidature and who, with Napoleon's approval, arranged for the Roumanian envoy in Paris to go direct to Sigmaringen and paint in the darkest colours the situation that was likely to confront Leopold in Spain. On July 11 Karl Anton made up his mind that his son's candidature must be withdrawn. On the 12th the decision was telegraphed to Prim, King William and Olozaga, and South German papers were informed that 'In order to restore to the Spanish government freedom of initiative, the hereditary prince withdraws his candidature for the throne, firmly determined not to let a family matter become a pretext for war.' The crisis appeared to be at an end and France, after so many setbacks, to have won a remarkable diplomatic victory. Even Thiers was delighted and declared that Sadowa was almost avenged. The sustained though risky diplomatic offensive engaged in by Napoleon and his advisers had been fully justified.

But it needed cool heads to play the diplomatic game with such issues at stake, and heads in Paris were still all too hot and inexperienced. Ollivier himself, anxious to be firm, had inserted in the government's statement in reply to an interpellation in the Legislative Body on July 6 a passage which to many seemed to resemble a first step to war rather than to negotiation. His foreign minister, the Duc de Gramont, who read this statement to the Chamber, was an anti-Prussian diplomat who had been in office for only six weeks and never before held ministerial responsibility; and both were susceptible to the pressure of a public opinion whose natural anxiety and new belligerence they themselves by their utterances had helped to arouse. Extremists both on the right and on the left among the deputies loudly declared that withdrawal of the candidature was not enough, and ministers feared that the cabinet would fall if they did not yield to this demand for something more. Moreover, there were recent examples which showed that princely candidatures might sometimes be revived.

Thus it was that Gramont, understandably but most unwisely, sought and obtained Napoleon's approval for a further and fatal *démarche*, the so-called demand for guarantees. Benedetti was instructed to obtain from King William a statement in which he publicly associated himself with Leopold's withdrawal and undertook not to sanction any renewal of his candidature. The momentous interview took place on July 13 when Benedetti met the King taking his morning walk in the park at Ems. William, surprised at this new demand when he regarded the affair as ended, told the ambassador that it was impossible for him to give an undertaking unlimited in time, and, when Benedetti became importunate, said he had nothing to add, politely raised his hat, and went on his way. Later he refused to grant Benedetti another audience to discuss the matter further.

This was to give Bismarck his opportunity. Profoundly vexed at the collapse of his Spanish schemes, feeling that Prussia in turn had been humiliated as she had not been since Austria had humbled her at Olmütz in 1850, Bismarck had returned to Berlin on the 12th. On the evening of the 13th he received a telegram from Ems recounting what had passed between Benedetti and the King. He immediately produced an abridged and simplified version in such a way as to convey the impression that relations with France had been sharply and decisively broken off—the King had refused to receive the French Ambassador. This version he had transmitted officially for publication in most European capitals. It was, as he intended, to be a red rag to the Gallic bull. On reading it, crowds in Berlin began to shout for war. In Paris the shouts rose to a new crescendo. The telegram was the 'échec', the slap in the face, that Ollivier and Gramont had feared. But it was not at first certain that it was official. Faced with the imminence of war, Napoleon and his ministers debated for hours, hesitated, as in July 1866, whether or not to mobilize, and toyed with the idea of a congress. But confirmation that the Ems telegram was official, and the influence of the war party in the Council, supported by the Empress who attended two of its meetings, turned the scales. On the morning of the 15th the Council of Ministers voted for war and later that day the government's request for an immediate war credit of 50 million francs was voted with enthusiasm in the Legislative Body by an immense majority. 'You see', Napoleon is said to have remarked, 'in what a situation a government can sometimes find itself. Even if we had no admissible reason for war, we should now be compelled to declare it, in order to obey the will of the country.'

Thus the 'inevitable' war was brought about unexpectedly in July 1870 and not at some later date deliberately planned by either party. An excitable public opinion, a timid government anxious to be firm and therefore committing inexcusable blunders, and a sense of fatality—that what had to come some time had better come now—carried the French people into a struggle that was to bring upon them unimagined catastrophes. Unfortunately, Gramont's demand for guarantees and Bismarck's exploitation of it had made France, the injured party on July 3, appear the unreasonable aggressor by July 13. Unfortunately, neither the nation nor its leaders had any conception of the kind of war they were confronted with. Leboeuf had assured the Legislative Body that the army was ready, and most Frenchmen confidently expected that it would soon be sweeping across the Rhine, as in 1859 it had swept into the plain of Lombardy. Napoleon, too, still hoped that Austrian and Italian aid would be forthcoming. Despite Austria's declaration of neutrality, negotiations were not broken off, and, once the French troops, victorious on the Rhine, appeared in

South Germany as 'liberators', he believed that the two powers might yet throw in their lot with France or at least offer armed mediation. But the French victories were not forthcoming.

The tragedy was that Napoleon and his generals, for all the shortcomings of army reform and for all the warnings they had received from men like their able and well-informed military attaché in Berlin, seemed to have regarded the campaign in front of them as another Crimean or Italian war. And for a war against an enemy such as Russia in 1854 or Austria in 1859 the French army was in fact ready and better equipped than before, for now, as a result of Napoleon's insistence, it was fully armed with the *chassepot*, which, military authorities generally agree, was a magnificent weapon. But the Prussia of 1870 was a very different foe, and from the outset French efforts were frustrated by confusion, error and uncertainty.

The first great error was Napoleon's own assumption of command. As in 1859, the Empress was appointed Regent to carry on the government in Paris, while the Emperor himself departed to command the armies, taking with him the Prince Imperial so that the boy could have his baptism of fire and be present at the first victories. Yet Napoleon had already demonstrated his incapacity for such a role in 1859. Now, eleven years older, often in excruciating pain, more than ever vacillating, he was doubly unfit. But he bore the name of Napoleon, and the strong pressure of the Empress convinced him that he must not shirk this task, however arduous it might be. The second error was Napoleon's 'almost casual' decision on the eve of hostilities to change the plan of army organization. Leboeuf had been making preparations, on the basis of a defensive plan drawn up in 1868, for the establishment of three armies, each under a marshal, at Châlons, Metz and Strasbourg. Napoleon, eager for an offensive and pursuing the will-of-the-wisp of the Austrian alliance, ordained that there should be a single army with his own headquarters at Metz and the three marshals, Bazaine, Canrobert and MacMahon under him, each in charge of larger army corps than usual. This change so late in the day gravely added to the difficulties of a mobilization which in any event was hampered by all manner of defects in organization.

Leboeuf was fully aware of the importance of speedy mobilization and had hoped to have the Army of the Rhine complete with 385,000 men at the end of a fortnight. But the general post of men moving from all over France, Algeria, and even Rome to join their regimental depots and concentration areas, added to the movements of stores and equipment, led to immense confusion. The railway lines were clogged, the ample supplies could not be distributed, and men lacked maps, equipment and even food. At the end of the fortnight the Army of the Rhine numbered less than 200,000. It was impossible to take the offensive and the commanders waited for inspiration and drive from the Emperor, who reached Metz on July 28, but was physically and mentally incapable of dominating the situation. An initial success near Saarbrücken was exaggerated in Paris as a notable victory, but four days later, on August 6, although they fought with great bravery, the French were defeated with heavy losses at Spicheren and at Froeschwiller in Alsace. Their cavalry was useless in face of breech-loading rifles and the Prussians displayed a shattering superiority in field artillery, partly because the French had too few of their own excellent new *mitrailleuses* and not enough men trained to handle them.

In Paris the news of these defeats, which opened the way to invasion, caused consternation and an explosion of rage, which was all the greater because a striking victory had falsely been reported the day before. There was an outcry against the government and even the regime itself. The recall of parliament was demanded and men on the Left called for the arming of Paris and the formation of a defence committee of Paris deputies, all Republicans. The recall of parliament was irresistible, but it meant the downfall of the cabinet which had led the country into war and not known how to give it victory. Only a handful of deputies supported Ollivier, whose government on August 9 was replaced by a more Right-wing ministry headed by a general. This at once took drastic measures for the defence of the country and the prosecution of the war, but many already believed that the days of the Empire were numbered.

When he heard the news from Paris, Napoleon commented

that he did not know 'what they are doing . . . They have lost their heads. . . . It is not in the midst of the storm that one changes one's pilot and crew.' But it was most unlikely that, even if parliament had not been recalled, Ollivier and the Empress could have weathered the storm and saved the Empire, for the crucial decisions were on the battlefield and there Napoleon himself had momentarily lost his head. The débâcle had already begun.

On the 7th, in a sudden panic, Napoleon had abandoned a plan of attack which Moltke himself was to commend and had ordered the whole army to fall back upon Châlons. The order was countermanded at Ollivier's instance, but it was clear that the Emperor could no longer bear the strain of command. He agreed to surrender his responsibilities, but the marshal he selected to succeed him was Bazaine and not Leboeuf, who, though probably the most capable man available, was now made by politicians the scapegoat of defeat. Bazaine knew he was unfit for such a post, but he was brave, popular and a man of the people, and the press and politicians clamoured for his nomination. Once again Napoleon bowed calamitously to public opinion.

Despite his relinquishment of the supreme command, Napoleon did not go back to Paris, for the Empress deemed that his return at such a juncture would provoke revolution and adjured him to remain with the army. So the unhappy sovereign, still treated as commander-in-chief by the reluctant Bazaine, adopted a compromise and himself went on August 16 in a third-class railway carriage to Châlons to organize a new army. But, once there, he became increasingly a cipher, at the mercy of conflicting advice from Paris, from visiting politicians, and from the generals on the spot. Meanwhile, defeat followed upon defeat. Outmanoeuvred, Bazaine was cut off in Metz, and MacMahon, now in effective command of the army at Châlons, was told by the government that, if he abandoned Bazaine, revolution would follow in Paris and he himself be attacked by the entire enemy forces. Political motives and ignorance at Paris thus obliged MacMahon against his better judgment to make the move that was to be his doom. With him went the Emperor, now a tragic encumbrance, unable to command, unable to govern, racked by pain and agonizing thoughts, yet impassive, physically courageous, and dignified to the end.

The last battle of his reign was fought at Sedan on August 31 and September 1. When all was over Napoleon wrote to Eugénie: 'I never dreamt of a catastrophe so appalling . . . Never will the sight of so terrible defeat be seen again.' He himself and MacMahon had been taken prisoner and with them an army of 84,000 men.

When the news reached Paris on September 4 a bloodless revolution swept the Empire away. Not a shot was fired in its defence, and in the Legislative Body only one voice was raised on its behalf. The Empress fled to England, unwept and almost unobserved. A Republic was proclaimed and new men took over the desperate task of continuing the war and averting total defeat. The prophecy of the great French thinker Tocqueville was being fulfilled: 'In war' the Second Empire 'will assuredly find its destruction; but perhaps its destruction will cost us very dear.'

Epilogue

NAPOLEON III spent seven months in captivity at Wilhelmshöhe in Germany. The Empress wrote to him suggesting that after his release they should settle in Trieste, but he replied: 'When I am free it is in England that I wish to live with you and Louis [the Prince Imperial], in a little cottage with bow windows and creeper.' The 'little cottage' selected by the Empress was, however, a Georgian mansion named Camden Place at Chislehurst in Kent. Hither the Emperor came after his release towards the end of March 1871 and here he was to stay with his wife and son and a small entourage of friends and servants for the short span of life that remained to him. He resumed his old occupations, writing again on military and other subjects—in particular a justification of his conduct of the army, *Les Forces Militaires de la France en 1870* —inspecting artillery batteries and inventions, discussing a plan for a permanent Council to settle international disputes, and even, in order to benefit poor people in bitter winters, himself designing a heating apparatus which would heat a room for half the normal cost.

Here, too, he waited and watched for favourable signs from France. Gradually they began to appear. The Republican Government of National Defence had gallantly prolonged the war for five months, but all in vain. A large part of the country had been occupied, Paris had been besieged, and then in March 1871 there had followed the fierce civil war of the Commune. Once again the peasantry's fears of socialism had been aroused and the future of the Republic was uncertain, since there was for a while a monarchist majority in the National Assembly. In these circumstances there were many of those who had voted

'Oui' in the plebiscite of 1870, particularly in rural areas or in Corsica, who regretted the Empire. Thus Napoleon's supporters took heart and a Bonapartist party re-emerged to work for a new restoration. A plan began to take shape for another Bonapartist coup. The Emperor was to depart secretly for Switzerland, don his general's uniform, cross into France and make for Lyons, where one of his former generals would raise the standard of revolt. A list of ministers was prepared and it was decided that, since the Tuileries had been burnt down in the Commune, the Emperor would reside in the Louvre. The day tentatively fixed for this new 'return from Elba' was March 20, 1873.

But in his heart of hearts Napoleon must have known that he would never set foot in France again. His illness grew rapidly worse in the second half of 1872 and two leading English doctors advised that a series of operations would be necessary. The patient consented, hoping against hope that all would be well and that he could ride his horse once more, but the strain was too great. On the morning of January 9, 1873, when he was due to have the third of these operations, Napoleon died. His last words, whispered to his ever faithful friend and doctor, Conneau, are said to have been 'Conneau, were you at Sedan?'

In this last hour men did not forget the Emperor's failings, his loose-living, his mendacity, his vacillations and the calamities which had ended his reign. But they also remembered the manifold improvements which he had brought to his country and to which the great German historian, von Sybel, amongst others paid eloquent tribute. Above all they remembered his goodness. Even *The Times*, so often one of his sharpest English opponents, acknowledged that 'Napoleon III had the qualities which win personal affection, respect, and admiration. He had genuine love and friendship; he was loyal to his friends; true to all who worked with him, had his full share of personal courage, and was most grateful to all who had ever done him even a small service . . . Received on these shores with the sympathy due to misfortune and followed everywhere with the respect due to a dignified bearing and affectionate nature, the Emperor acquires a new claim to consideration in the agonies of his deathbed, the manly patience with which they have been borne, and the deep affliction of those he leaves behind him.'

A Brief Note on Books

1. *Bibliographies.* The older literature is well surveyed in R. Schnerb, 'Napoleon III and the French Second Empire' (*Journal of Modern History*, Sept. 1936) and in F. A. Simpson's *The Rise of Louis Napoleon* (3rd edn., London, 1950) and *Louis Napoleon and the Recovery of France* (3rd edn., London, 1951). More up-to-date guides are to be found in J. Droz, L. Genet and J. Vidalenc, *L'époque contemporaine: I. Restorations et Révolutions 1815–71* (Clio series, Paris, 1953); G. P. Gooch, *The Second Empire* (London, 1960); and T. A. B. Corley, *Democratic Despot. A Life of Napoleon III* (London, 1961).

2. *Napoleon III's own writings.* A number of the main writings and speeches are collected in *Oeuvres de Napoléon III* (5 vols., Paris, 1869). These include *Des idées Napoléoniennes* and *L'Extinction du Paupérisme*, but not *La Vie de Jules César* (1866). No complete collection exists of Napoleon's letters and those that have been published are widely scattered. Some of the most important are to be found in the following: M. Emerit, *Lettres de Napoléon III à Madame Cornu* (2 vols., Paris, 1937); B. Jerrold, *The Life of Napoleon III* (4 vols., London, 1874–82); R. H. Edleston, *Napoléon III. Speeches from the Throne* ... (Cambridge, 1931); *Il Carteggio Cavour-Nigra del 1858 al 1861* (4 vols., Bologna, 1920–29); E. d'Hauterive, *The Second Empire and its Downfall* (London, 1927); *Les Origines diplomatiques de la guerre de 1870–71* (29 vols., Paris, 1910–30); E. Ollivier, *L'Empire Libéral* (18 vols., Paris, 1895–1918).

3. *Memoirs and conversations.* These are numerous. Particularly valuable are the memoirs and records of British and Austrian ambassadors, especially the extracts from the Cowley

papers edited by Sir V. Wellesley and R. Sencourt under the title of *Conversations with Napoleon III* (London, 1934); Graf A. von Hübner, *Neuf ans de souvenirs . . . 1851–1859* (Paris, 1904); and Lord Newton, *Lord Lyons, A Record of British Diplomacy* (2 vols., London, 1913). This last relates to the years 1867–70.

4. *General.* There are many general histories in French and several in English. Apart from F. A. Simpson's unfinished work, mentioned in §1 above, the more notable recent studies in English are A. L. Guérard's *Napoleon III* (Cambridge, Mass., 1943); J. M. Thompson's *Louis Napoleon and the Second Empire* (Oxford, 1954); and T. A. B. Corley's book mentioned in §1 above. All these are sympathetic to their subject. J. M. Thompson's book is written with distinction and critical insight, while T. A. B. Corley's is based on a wide reading of recent specialized literature and shows particular awareness of economic problems.

In French the classic history is P. de la Gorce's *Histoire du Second Empire* (7 vols., 4th edn., Paris, 1899). This work of a Catholic historian is to be contrasted with C. Seignobos's useful but more matter-of-fact treatment in Vols. VI and VII of E. Lavisse's *Histoire de France contemporaine* (Paris, 1921). Three admirable, highly condensed, more recent assessments are M. Blanchard's *Le Second Empire* (Collection Armand Colin, Paris, 1950); L. Girard's chapter in Vol. 2 of the superbly illustrated Larousse's *Histoire de France* (ed. M. Reinhard, Paris, 1954); and G. Pradalié's *Le Second Empire* ('Que sais-je?' series, Paris, 1957). S. Desternes and H. Chandet's *Napoléon III homme du XXe Siècle* (Paris, 1961) is popularly written, but uses some interesting material previously unpublished.

Finally, the reader who enjoys pictorial impressions will be rewarded if he can come by a copy of A. Dayot's album, *Le Second Empire, 1851–1870* (Paris, s.d.) or of J. M. Haswell's *Napoleon III from the Popular Caricatures of the Last 30 Years* (London, 1871).

Apart from these, the following are a few of the many books particularly relevant to individual chapters in this volume:

a. *Chapter I.* E. de Budé, *Les Bonaparte en Suisse* (Geneva, 1905), is based on Swiss sources. Ivor Guest's *Napoleon in*

England (London, 1952) is a fascinating book. M. de La Fuye and E. A. Babeau's *Louis Napoléon Bonaparte avant l'Empire* (Paris, 1951) is the most recent study in French of the Emperor's early career.

b. *Chapter II.* The Napoleonic legend was brilliantly surveyed many years ago in H. A. L. Fisher's *Bonapartism* (Oxford, 1908). Its growth has been subjected to a detailed examination in J. Lucas-Dubreton's *Le Culte de Napoléon 1815–1848* (Paris, 1960). An authoritative book on the ideas and institutions of the Second Republic is P. Bastid, *Doctrines et institutions politiques de la Seconde République* (Paris, 1945). On the *coup d'état* H. Guillemin's *Le coup du 2 décembre* (Paris, 1952) is hostile, the Earl of Kerry's, *The Secret of the Coup d'Etat* (London, 1924) contains important documents.

c. *Chapter III.* The text of the constitutions of 1848 and of 1852 may conveniently be found in J. P. T. Bury, *France 1814–1940* (3rd edn. amended, London, 1959). T. Zeldin's *The Political System of Napoleon III* (London, 1958) is interesting on parties and electoral management. I. Collins's *The Government and the Newspaper Press in France 1814–1881* (Oxford, 1951) is an excellent survey of government control of the press. There is no thorough history of the police or up-to-date study of the army, but R. Girardet, *La Société Militaire dans la France contemporaine (1815–1939)* (Paris, 1953) is illuminating about the mentality of the army and its place in society. On the other hand, Napoleon III's policy towards the Church has been impressively examined by J. Maurain in *La politique ecclésiastique du Second Empire de 1852 à 1869* (Paris, 1930). Many of his findings were conveniently summarized in C. S. Phillips, *The Church in France 1848–1907* (London, 1936).

d. *Chapter IV.* J. H. Clapham's *The Economic Development of France and Germany, 1815–1914* (Cambridge, 1921) is still useful. A Dutch study, H. N. Boon's *Rêve et Réalité dans l'oeuvre économique et sociale de Napoléon III* (The Hague, 1936), is of interest for Napoleon's ideas on economic and social policy. The oustanding book on the public works of the reign is L. Girard's *La Politique des Travaux Publics du Second Empire* (Paris, 1952). France's economic expansion in Europe has been comprehensively surveyed in Rondo E. Cameron, *France and the Economic Development of Europe 1800–1914* (Princeton, 1961). The transformation of Paris has inspired an absorbing study by David H. Pinkney, *Napoleon III and the Rebuilding of Paris* (Princeton, 1958). The main work on Napoleon's free trade policy is still A. L. Dunham, *The Anglo-French Treaty of Commerce of 1860 and the Progress of the Industrial Revolution in France* (University of Michigan Press, 1930).

e. *Chapter V.* The general complexities of European diplomacy have been unravelled in stimulating fashion by A. J. P. Taylor in *The Struggle for Mastery in Europe* (Oxford, 1960). The main phases of Napoleon's foreign policy have been expounded with admirable lucidity by P. Renouvin in his *Histoire Extérieure du Second Empire* (a cyclostyled course of lectures given at the Sorbonne, Paris, s.d.). Aspects of Napoleon III's relations with England have been examined by F. C. Palm, *England and Napoleon III* (Durham, N.C., 1948). The history of the Crimean War is fully treated in H. Temperley, *The Crimea* (London, 1936) and excellently summarized in Miss A. Ramm's chapter in *The New Cambridge Modern History*, Vol. X (Cambridge, 1960). The influence of public opinion has been assessed in L. M. Case's important *French Opinion in War and Diplomacy during the Second Empire* (Philadelphia, 1954).

f. *Chapter VI.* In addition to the books already mentioned in §c the following may be of interest: R. Schnerb's authoritative study of *Rouher et le Second Empire* (Paris, 1949); G. Duveau's massive *La vie ouvrière en France sous le Second Empire* (Paris, 1946); G. Weill's standard *Histoire du Parti Républicain en France (1814–1870)* and T. Zeldin's succinct *Emile Ollivier and the Liberal Empire of Napoleon III* (Oxford, 1963).

g. *Chapter VII.* In addition to the books mentioned in §e, P. Henry, *Napoléon III et les Peuples* (Gap, 1943), examines Napoleon's attitude to nationalities. An able survey of some of the main diplomatic issues is W. E. Mosse's *The European Powers and the German Question 1848–71* (Cambridge, 1958).

h. *Chapter VIII.* There is no detailed general survey of

Napoleon's colonial policy. A useful general book on French colonial enterprise is, however, H. Blet, *Histoire de la Colonisation Française* (Vol. II, Paris, 1946). Napoleon's Algerian policies have been reviewed in E. H. Cordier, *Napoléon III et l'Algérie* (Algiers, 1937) and his policy in the Far East has been surveyed in John F. Cady, *The Roots of French Imperialism in Eastern Asia* (Cornell University Press, 1954). The main study of Napoleon III's Mexican policy is C. Schefer's *La grande pensée de Napoléon III: Les origines de l'expédition de Mexique 1858–62* (Paris, 1939).

i. *Chapter IX*. In addition to the books already listed, mention must be made of Ollivier's immense and finely written *L'Empire Libéral* (see §2).

j. *Chapter X*. A thorough study of French army reform after 1866 is J. Casevitz's *Une loi manquée: la loi Niel (1866–1868)* (c. 1959). The main apologia for French policy in the Hohenzollern candidature crisis is in Ollivier's *L'Empire Libéral* (see under Chapter IX). The crisis itself has been re-examined in L. D. Steefel's admirable *Bismarck, the Hohenzollern Candidacy and the Origins of the Franco-German War of 1870* (Cambridge, Mass., 1962). Finally, the course of the war of 1870 has been brilliantly described in M. Howard's *The Franco-Prussian War* (London, 1961).

Index